Drew Provan

iPhone

in easy steps

covers iOS 8

5th edition updated for iPhone 6 and 6 Plus

1 The iPhone 6 and iPhone 6 Plus

The latest iPhone comes in two models; the iPhone 6 and the iPhone 6 Plus. They are both sophisticated and highly capable smartphones which are able to make calls, send texts and multimedia messages, browse the web, take and store videos and still photos, play games and keep you organized professionally and personally.

The iPhone 6 and iPhone 6 Plus both have similar storage options (they both come in 16GB, 64GB and 128GB models) and have an 8 megapixel iSight camera and an A8 chip processor. The main difference between the two is the weight and the screen sizes.

Because the iPhone 6 and iPhone 6 Plus are generally the same, other than their size and weight, they will both be referred to as iPhone 6, or just iPhone, unless required otherwise.

The New icon pictured above indicates a new or enhanced feature introduced with the iPhone 6 with iOS 8.

A Very Smart Smartphone!

Apple's first generation iPhone was launched in June 2007. Because of the advance publicity there was a feeding frenzy when launch day came, with customers queuing for many hours to get their hands on an iPhone.

There were several reasons for the excitement, including the Apple brand (stylish, functional and innovative). People already loved the iPod so a cell phone with iPod capabilities and a wide screen had major appeal. The sheer simplicity of operation, using a touchscreen rather than a plethora of buttons, had major appeal.

So this was a cell phone unlike any other. In addition to the usual telephony capabilities, this phone could play music, videos, YouTube and more. It could be used as a diary with easy synchronization to Microsoft Outlook or Apple Calendar. It would handle email (including Exchange Server) more easily. Its SMS app made messaging a breeze. Its browser made browsing the web easier than with previous smartphones.

In addition, there were apps such as Weather, Stocks, Maps and others. Despite criticisms from some quarters regarding the poor camera (2 megapixels in the first and second generation iPhones) and lack of video, along with the inability for the user to add more apps, the first generation iPhone was a huge success.

The second generation iPhone was launched in July 2008 and brought with it 3G, a much faster data network connection. In June 2009 the 3GS ("S" stands for "speed") was launched. The new iPhone 3GS brought with it the ability to capture video, Voice Control, which enables users to control the iPhone 3GS using voice commands, and numerous other features.

The 4G iPhone was launched in June 2010 and brought with it many refinements such as dual cameras, camera flash, FaceTime, Siri, higher resolution Retina Display screen and many other improvements over the previous models. The 4GS was launched in Summer 2011, and September 2012 saw the arrival of iPhone 5 with the iPhone 5C and 5S following a year later.

The iPhone 6 was launched in September 2014 and comes in the standard iPhone 6 model and also the iPhone 6 Plus, which has a larger screen. Both models are thinner and lighter than their predecessors and have retina HD screens: 4.7 inches for the iPhone 6 and 5.5 inches for the iPhone 6 Plus.

What Does It Do?

It would be easier to ask what it *doesn't* do! The iPhone, even as a basic cell phone, before you start adding applications, has many functions – probably enough for most people without actually having to add more apps of your own. But, since there are *thousands* of applications available for download, you can extend the functionality of the iPhone way beyond this. The iPhone is more like a small computer since you can store files, email, connect to other desktop computers, view documents including Word and PDF files, play games, look up recipes, manage your time, and many other functions.

Hot tip

The iPhone is more like a computer than a standard cell phone.

Apps for work and play   Camera   On/Off button

Settings to customize your iPhone   App Store for more apps

Don't forget

Press and hold the On/Off button to turn on the iPhone, or access the screen for turning it off. Press it once to put the iPhone into Sleep mode, or to wake it up from Sleep mode.

iPhone 6 Specifications

Cellular and wireless capabilities

The iPhone 6 is a Quad band phone which uses GSM and GPRS/EDGE.

There is also built-in Wi-Fi (802.11a/b/g/n/ac) and Bluetooth 4.0. The iPhone also includes Global Positioning System (GPS) software, making it easy to geotag (see page 42) your pictures and videos. iPhone 6 also uses 3G and 4G networks where available.

Battery

Unlike most cell phones, the user cannot take the battery out for replacement. The iPhone uses a built-in battery which is charged using a USB connection to the computer, or using the lightning charger supplied by Apple.

What do you get from a full charge?

- Talk time: Up to 14 hours on 3G

- Standby time: Up to 10 days (250 hours)

- Internet use: Up to 10 hours on 3G, up to 11 hours Wi-Fi

- Video playback: Up to 11 hours

- Audio playback: Up to 50 hours

Internal storage

The iPhone uses internal flash drive storage. There is no SD or other card slot so the internal flash memory is all the storage you have – use it wisely!

iPhone 6 is available with 16GB, 64GB or 128GB storage capacity.

In terms of color, you can get the iPhone 6 in Silver, Gold or Space Gray.

You cannot remove the iPhone battery. This has to be carried out by Apple.

If you intend to keep videos as well as music on your iPhone it may be wise to opt for the higher capacity iPhone.

What can I do with the storage space?

	16GB	64GB	128GB
Songs:	3,500	14,000	28,000
Videos:	20 hour	80 hours	160 hours
Photos:	20,000	50,000	100,000

Beware

The amount of storage space for songs, videos and photos can vary depending on the way the content has been created, particularly for videos and photos.

Sensors in the iPhone

There are four sensors in the iPhone: the Three-Axis Gyro, the Accelerometer, Proximity Sensor and the Ambient Light Sensor.

The *Accelerometer* enables the phone to detect rotation and position. This is important when switching from portrait to landscape viewing. The Accelerometer is also used in many of the iPhone game apps such as *Labyrinth* (below) which uses the Accelerometer to good effect – as you tilt the iPhone, the ball bearing moves across a virtual board.

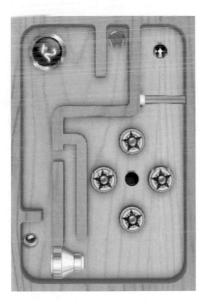

The *Proximity Sensor* switches off the iPhone screen when you make a call – it senses that the phone is close to the ear, saving valuable power. The *Ambient Light Sensor* adjusts the iPhone screen to the ambient lighting, again saving energy if a bright screen is not required.

The iPhone Itself

Unlike some cell phones, the iPhone is unusual since it has very few physical buttons.

Buttons you need to know on the iPhone

- Sleep/Wake (On/Off)
- Ring/Silent
- Volume controls
- Home button

Press the Sleep/Wake (On/Off) button as soon as you have finished using the iPhone – this helps conserve battery power, by putting it into Sleep mode. Press the button again to wake up the iPhone.

On/Off/Sleep/Wake up, on the right side of the body

Ring/Silent on the left side

Volume controls on the left side

Home button

Sleep/Wake

Press and briefly hold this button if your iPhone is switched off. You will see the Apple logo and the loading screen will start up. You will then be taken to the Home screen, also known as Homepage (opposite page). If you wish to put your phone away, press the Sleep/Wake button to put your phone to sleep.

Ring/Silent

You often want your phone on silent, during meetings for example. The Ring/Silent button can be toggled up and down. When you see the red line, this means the iPhone is on silent.

Pressing the Home button takes you back to the Home screen from any app you are using.

The Home button

This does what the name suggests and brings you back to the Home screen from wherever you are. If you are browsing applications in another screen, pressing the Home button will bring you right back to the Home screen. If you are using an app, pressing Home will close the app. If you are on a phone call, pressing the Home button lets you access your email or other apps.

On the iPhone 6 the Home button can also be used as a fingerprint sensor for unlocking the phone with your unique fingerprint (see page 53).

13

Other Buttons on the iPhone

Volume controls

Volume is controlled using two separate buttons – a **+** and **−** button (increase and decrease volume respectively). You can easily adjust the volume of the audio output when you are listening to the Music app, or when you are making a phone call. If you cannot hear the caller very well try increasing the volume.

There are no visual symbols on the volume buttons: the volume down button is below the volume up button.

14

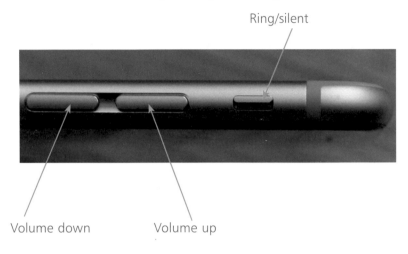

Ring/silent

Volume down   Volume up

The Nano SIM slot

The iPhone 6 uses a nano SIM (much smaller than micro SIM which is used in older iPhone models). Apple provides a SIM removal tool in the iPhone box.

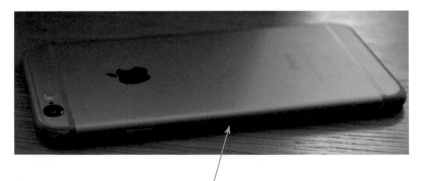

Insert the SIM tool into this hole and push it firmly. The SIM card holder will pop out and you can remove it and insert a SIM card

Lightning connector, speaker, microphone, and headset jack
These are located at the bottom of the iPhone.

Headset jack   Lightning connector

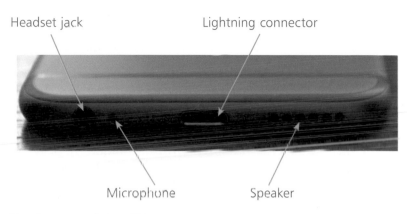

Microphone   Speaker

Back view of the iPhone 6
This shows the location of the main camera and the LED flash
(flash is not available for the front camera).

LED flash (and torch)

Rear microphone

iSight camera

15

Setting up Your iPhone

Before you can do anything on your iPhone you will need to activate it.

Once you switch on the new iPhone 6 (press the On/Off button) you will be taken through a series of screens where you set up various options.

Even though the initial setup is carried out wirelessly, you should plug your iPhone 6 into iTunes on your Mac or PC regularly to make sure you have a recent backup of the iPhone in case you lose or damage the iPhone.

Initially, there will be a series of setup screens to move through before you can use the iPhone. These include the following options (a lot of these can be skipped during the setup and accessed later from the **Settings** app):

- **Language.** Select the language you want to use.

- **Country.** Select your current country or region.

- **Wi-Fi network.** Select a Wi-Fi network to connect to the Internet. If you are at home, this will be your own Wi-Fi network, if available. If you are at a Wi-Fi hotspot then this will appear on your network list.

  ### Choose a Wi-Fi Network

  ‹ Back

  NETGEAR   🔒 📶 ›

  virginmedia6249958   🔒 📶 ›

  Choose another network

- **Location Services.** This determines whether your iPhone can use your geographical location for apps that use this type of information (such as Maps).

  ‹ Back

  ### Location Services

  Enable Location Services   ›

  Disable Location Services   ›

- **Set Up iPhone.** You can use this to set up your iPhone from scratch, or restore it from a backup that has been created via iCloud or on iTunes.

- **Apple ID.** You can register with this to be able to access a range of Apple facilities, such as iCloud, purchase items on iTunes or the App Store, FaceTime, Messages and iBooks. You can also create an Apple ID whenever you first access one of the relevant apps (see page 32).

- **iCloud.** This is Apple's online service for sharing and backing up content. See pages 32-41 for details.

- **Find My iPhone.** This is a service that can be activated so that you can locate your iPhone If it is lost or stolen. This is done via the online ICloud site at **www.icloud.com**

- **Touch ID.** This can be used on the iPhone 6 to create a fingerprint ID that can be used to unlock the phone.

- **Create a Passcode.** This can be used to create a four digit code for unlocking the phone. This step can be skipped if required.

- **Siri** This is the voice assistant that can be used to find things on your iPhone and on the Web.

- **Diagnostic information.** This enables information about your iPhone to be sent to Apple.

- **Display Zoom.** This can be used to increase the size of the display so that the icons are larger.

- **Get Started.** Once the setup process has been completed you can start using your iPhone.

The Home Screen

What's on the Home screen?

When you turn the iPhone on you will see some icons which are fixed, such as the top bar with the time and battery charge indicator, as well as the Dock at the bottom which holds four apps. By default, your iPhone will have Phone, Mail, Safari and Music on the bottom Dock. You can move these off the Dock if you want, but Apple puts these here because they are the most commonly-used apps, and having them on the Dock makes them easy to find.

Just above the Dock you will see two dots. The dots represent each of your screens – the more apps you install, the more screens you will need to accommodate them (you are allowed 11 in all). The illustration here shows an iPhone with two screens, and the Home screen is the one we are viewing. If you flicked to the next screen, the second dot would be white and the first one would be black. In effect, these are meant to let you know where you are at any time.

Beware

As you download more apps from the App Store these will be placed on subsequent Home screens, as each one gets filled up.

Beware

The Battery indicator is fairly crude. For a more accurate guide, try switching on Battery % in Settings.

Signal strength, network and Wi-Fi   Bluetooth icon   Battery

Default apps (which can be moved around but not deleted)

Dots representing the number of screens. Tap on a dot to move to that screen, or swipe left and right to move between screens

The Dock, where apps can be placed and appear on all screens

Default Applications

The iPhone comes with applications that are part of the operating system. The core set here cannot be deleted.

Messages

Notes

Calendar

Photos

Calculator

Clock

Camera

Settings

Maps

iTunes Store

Phone

Weather

Stocks

App Store

Mail

Voice Memos

Safari

Game Center

Music

Videos

Newsstand

Reminders

Contacts

Health

NEW

iBooks

Podcasts

The apps for iBooks and Podcasts previously had to be downloaded from the App Store, but in iOS 8 they come preinstalled, as does a new Tips app for getting help on a variety of different topics.

The iPhone Dock

By default, there are four apps on the Dock at the bottom of the screen. These are the four that Apple thinks you will use most frequently:

- **Phone**, for calls

- **Mail**, for email

- **Safari**, for web browsing

- **Music**

You can rearrange the order in which the Dock apps appear:

 Tap and hold on one of the Dock apps until it starts to jiggle

 Drag the app into its new position

 Click once on the **Home** button to return from edit mode

Just above the Dock is a line of small white dots. These indicate how many screens of content there are on the iPhone. Tap on one of the dots to go to that screen.

...cont'd

Adding and removing Dock apps

You can also remove apps from the Dock and add new ones:

 To remove an app from the Dock tap and hold it and drag it onto the main screen area

 To add an app to the Dock tap and hold it and drag it onto the Dock

 The number of items that can be added to the Dock is restricted to a maximum of four as the icons do not resize

 Click once on the **Home** button to return from edit mode

If items are removed from the Dock they are still available in the same way from the main screen.

Software Version iOS 8

iOS 8 is the latest version of the operating system for the iPhone (and also the iPad and iPod Touch) and it brings in many new features and functions.

iOS 8 is an evolutionary development of iOS 7, which was one of the most dramatic cosmetic changes to the operating system in its history. It produced a flatter, cleaner design and this has been continued with iOS 8, which is not greatly different in appearance to its predecessor.

Linking it all up

One of the features of iOS 8 is the way it links up with other Apple devices, whether it is something like an iPad also using iOS 8, or an Apple desktop or laptop computer running the OS X Yosemite operating system. This works with apps such as Mail and Photos, so you can start an email on one device and finish it on another, or take a photo on one device and have it available on all other compatible Apple devices. Most of this is done through iCloud and once it is set up it takes care of most

of these tasks automatically. (See pages 32-41 for details about setting up and using iCloud, Family Sharing and iCloud Drive.)

Close

Family Sharing

Family Sharing is the easy way to share what's important with members of your family.

Get Started

Share purchased music, movies, books, and eligible apps.

Share photos and videos in a family photo stream.

New and improved apps

Several of the iOS 8 apps have been updated and improved: the Messages app now enables group texts, video messages and displaying your locations; the Photos app has increased sharing capabilities; the Camera app now has a time-lapse option; and the keyboard has an option for using predictive text. There is also a new Tips app and the iBooks and Podcasts apps are now preinstalled, saving the need to download them from the App Store. Another new feature is the Health app, which enables you to keep track of a wide range of health and fitness issues and log the relevant data which is then stored and analyzed by the app.

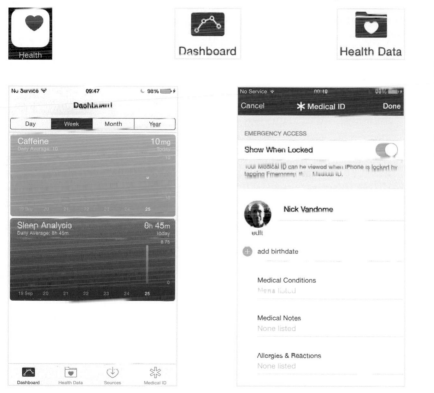

For more details on using the new Health app, see Chapter Six.

iOS 8 is an operating system that is stylish and versatile on the iPhone 6 and it also plays an important role in the holy grail of computing: linking desktop and mobile devices so that users can spend more time doing the things that matter to them, safe in the knowledge that their content will be backed up and available across multiple devices.

23

The iPhone 6 has a 4.7 inch screen and the iPhone 6 Plus has the larger, 5.5 inch, screen.

Although the iPhone has a fingerprint-resistant coating it still gets grubby. A number of companies make screen protectors and can also protect the other parts of the iPhone from scratching by using a protective case.

The Touch Screen Display

The iPhone uses a touch-sensitive screen for input, using gestures and a virtual keyboard. The screen is 4.7 or 5.5 inches (diagonal) and has a resolution of 1136 x 750-pixel resolution at 326 PPI (Pixels Per Inch), or 1920 x 1080 at 401 PPI. Apple has called this the *Retina Display* because the resolution is so high. This results in great clarity when viewing the browser or watching movies on the iPhone.

Touch screen features
The screen is able to detect touch using skin, using these gestures.

Tapping
Tapping with one finger is used for lots of apps. It's a bit like clicking with the mouse. You tap apps to open them, to open hyperlinks, to select photo albums which then open, to enter text using the keyboard, and many other tasks.

Sliding
You also use the slide action to answer phone calls, shut down the iPhone and unlock the Lock screen.

Dragging
This is used to move documents that occupy more than a screen's worth across the screen. Maps use this feature, as do web pages. Place your finger on the screen, keep it there and move the image to where you want it.

Pinching and spreading
To zoom in on a photo, web page or map, swipe outwards with thumb and forefinger. Pinch inwards to zoom back out.

Minimizing the screen
One feature of the iPhone 6 is to make everything easily within reach. This can be done by minimizing the screen to enable you to use it with one hand. To do this, double-tap gently on the Home button.

Flicking

If you are faced with a long list, e.g. in Contacts, you can flick the list up or down by placing your finger at the bottom or top of the screen, keeping your finger on the screen, then flicking your finger downwards or upwards and the list will fly up or down.

Shake the iPhone

When entering text or copying and pasting, to undo what you have done, shake the iPhone. Shake again to redo.

Portrait or landscape mode

The iPhone is generally viewed in a portrait mode but for many tasks it is easier to turn the iPhone and work in landscape mode. If you're in Mail, or using Safari, the text will be larger. More importantly, the keys of the virtual keyboard will become larger making it easier to type accurately.

Entering text

The iPhone has predictive text, but this is unlike any you may have used before. The accuracy is astonishing. As you type, the iPhone will make suggestions before you complete a word. If you agree with the suggested word, tap the spacebar. If you disagree, tap the small "x" next to the word.

You can shake your iPhone to skip audio tracks, undo and redo text, and more.

To accept a spelling suggestion tap the spacebar. Reject the suggestion by clicking the "x". Over time your iPhone will learn new words.

Cancel	**Visit**	Send
To: Eilidh Vandome		
Cc/Bcc, From: nickvandome@me.com		
Subject: **Visit**		

Do you still want to go to york

York ×

Sent from my iPhone

Q	W	E	R	T	Y	U	I	O	P
A	S	D	F	G	H	J	K	L	
⬆	Z	X	C	V	B	N	M	⌫	
123	☺	⚲	space	return					

Accept the capitalized word by tapping the spacebar

Cancel	**Visit**	Send
To: Eilidh Vandome		
Cc/Bcc, From: nickvandome@me.com		
Subject: **Visit**		

Do you still want to go to York tomorrow or perhaps you dont

don't ×

Sent from my iPhone

Q	W	E	R	T	Y	U	I	O	P
A	S	D	F	G	H	J	K	L	
⬆	Z	X	C	V	B	N	M	⌫	
123	☺	⚲	space	return					

Accept the apostrophe by tapping the spacebar

Double-tap the spacebar to insert a period followed by a space, ready for the next sentence to begin.

Multitasking Window

The iPhone can run several programs at once and these can be managed by the Multitasking window. This has been redesigned so it can also show your recent contacts at the top of the screen.

- It shows open apps

- It enables you to move between open apps and open different ones

- It enables apps to be closed (see next page)

Accessing Multitasking

The Multitasking option can be accessed from any screen on your iPhone, as follows:

1 Double-click on the **Home** button

2 The currently-open apps are displayed, with their icons underneath them (except the Home screen). The most recently-used apps are shown first

3 Swipe left and right to view the open apps. Tap on one to access it in full screen size

At the top of the Multitasking window are your most recent contacts and also any favorites you have assigned in the Contacts app. Tap on any of these to phone them, send them a text message or a FaceTime call.

The Multitasking window is also known as the App Switcher.

Closing Items

The iPhone deals with open apps very efficiently. They do not interact with other apps, which increases security and also means that they can be open in the background, without using up a significant amount of processing power, in a state of semi-hibernation until they are needed. Because of this it is not essential to close apps when you move to something else. However, you may want to close apps if you feel you have too many open or if one stops working. To do this:

 Access the Multitasking window. The currently-open apps are displayed

 Press and hold on an app and swipe it to the top of the screen to close it. This does not remove it from the iPhone and it can be opened again in the usual way

 The app is removed from its position in the Multitasking window

When you switch from one app to another, the first one stays open in the background. You can go back to it by accessing it from the Multitasking window or the Home screen.

In the Control Center

The Control Center is a panel containing some of the most commonly used options within the **Settings** app. It can be accessed with one swipe and is an excellent function for when you do not want to have to go into Settings.

Accessing the Control Center

The Control Center can be accessed from any screen within iOS 8 and it can also be accessed from the Lock Screen:

 Tap on the **Settings** app

 Tap on the **Control Center** tab and drag the **Access on Lock Screen** and **Access Within Apps** buttons On or Off to specify if the Control Center can be accessed from here (if both are Off, it can still be accessed from any Home screen)

3 Swipe up from the bottom of any screen to access the Control Center panel

4 Tap on this button to hide the Control Center panel, or tap anywhere on the screen

5 Use this slider to control the screen brightness

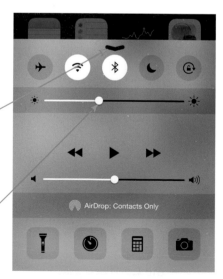

Beware

The Control Center cannot be disabled from being accessed from the Home screen.

...cont'd

Control Center controls

The items that can be used in the Control Center are:

1 Use these controls for any music or video that is playing. Use the buttons to Pause/Play a track, go to the beginning or end and adjust the volume

2 Tap on this button to turn **Airplane mode** On or Off

3 Tap on this button to turn **Wi-Fi** On or Off

4 Tap on this button to turn **Bluetooth** On or Off

5 Tap on this button to turn **Do Not Disturb** mode On or Off

6 Tap on this button to **Lock** or **Unlock** screen rotation. If it is locked, the screen will not change when you change the orientation of your iPhone

7 Tap on this button to activate the iPhone's **Torch**

8 Tap on this button to access a **Clock**, including a stopwatch

9 Tap on this button to open the **Calculator** app

10 Tap on this button to open the **Camera** app

When Airplane mode is activated the network and wireless connectivity on the iPhone is disabled. However, it can still be used for functions such as playing music or reading books.

29

The Torch function is very effective, particularly over short distances.

The Virtual Keyboard

The keys are small but when you touch them they become larger, which increases accuracy. The letter "T" below has been pressed and has become much larger.

Hot tip

The iPhone has done away with virtually all buttons and provides a software-based QWERTY keyboard. The keyboard becomes visible automatically when needed. When you press on a key it becomes expanded so that you can see it more clearly.

There are all the usual features of a computer keyboard, including

spacebar, delete key , shift , numbers and symbols .

To correct a word, touch the word you want to correct and hold your finger on the word. You will see a magnifying glass. Move your finger to where you want the insertion point (|) to be, stop there and delete any wrong letters.

Hot tip

Some keys such as Currency and URL endings can be accessed by holding down the key. A pop-up will show the options.

The keyboard has automatic spellcheck and correction of misspelled words. It has a dynamic dictionary (learns new words). Some keys have multiple options if you hold them down, e.g. hold down the $ key and you'll see the other characters.

Where's Caps Lock?

It is frustrating hitting the Caps key for every letter if you want to type a complete word in upper case. But you can activate Caps Lock easily:

- Go to **Settings > General**

- Select **Keyboard**

- Make sure the **Enable Caps Lock** slider is set to **On**

- While you are there, make sure the other settings are on, for example "**.**" **Shortcut** – this helps you add a period (full stop) by tapping the spacebar twice

It's a good idea to activate Caps Lock. To use, just tap Shift twice – the shift button should have a black, upwards pointing arrow on it with a black bar underneath it if you have activated it properly in the Settings.

No Service 🔋	12:53	⌞ ⊛ ▭+
‹ Settings	General	
Usage		›
Background App Refresh		›
Auto-Lock	1 Minute	›
Restrictions	Off	›
Date & Time		›
Keyboard		›
Language & Region		›
iTunes Wi-Fi Sync		›
VPN	Not Connected	›
Reset		›

No Service 🔋	12:53	⌞ ⊛ ▭+
‹ General	Keyboards	
Keyboards		2 ›
Shortcuts		›
Auto-Capitalization		⬤▭
Auto-Correction		⬤▭
Check Spelling		⬤▭
Enable Caps Lock		⬤▭
Predictive		▭⬤
"." Shortcut		⬤▭

Double tapping the space bar will insert a period followed by a space.

If you do not like the default iPhone keyboard, you can download third-party ones from the App Store. Some to look at include, SwiftKey, Swype and KuaiBoard.

Other settings for the keyboard

- **Auto-Correction** suggests the correct word. If it annoys you, switch it off

- **Auto-Capitalization** is great for putting capitals in names

- Whilst the "**.**" **Shortcut** types a period every time you hit the spacebar twice and saves time when typing long emails, if you prefer not to use this, you can switch it off. Here's another neat trick – you can also insert a period by tapping the spacebar with two fingers simultaneously

iCloud and an Apple ID

Apple iCloud

This is a service that allows you to use the cloud to sync your data (calendars, contacts, mail, Safari bookmarks, and notes) wirelessly.

Once you are registered and set up, any entries or deletions to calendars and other apps are reflected in all devices using iCloud.

An Apple ID is required for using iCloud, and this can be obtained online at **https://appleid.apple.com/** or you can create an Apple ID when you first access an app on your iPhone that requires this for use. It is free to create an Apple ID and requires a username and password. Once you have created an Apple ID you can then use the full range of iCloud services.

Start using iCloud on the iPhone and computers

The iPhone apps that require an Apple ID to access their full functionality include: iTunes Store, App Store, Messages, iBooks, Game Center and FaceTime.

1 Open the iCloud System Preferences (Mac) or Control Panel (PC)

2 Log into your iCloud account with your Apple ID (you only need to do this once – it will remember your details)

3 Check **On** the items that you want synced by iCloud

Using iCloud removes the need to sync items such as contacts, calendars, notes and photos on other iCloud-enabled devices that you have, such as tablets and computers: iCloud does it all automatically.

4 On your iPhone, open the **Settings > iCloud** and select the items you want to be used by iCloud. All of the selected items will be reflected on the equivalent apps on your computer

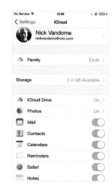

...cont'd

Using iCloud online

Once you have created an Apple ID you will automatically have an iCloud account. This can be used to sync your data from your iPhone and you can also access your content online from the iCloud website at **www.icloud.com**

 Enter your Apple ID details

 Click on the **iCloud** button from any section to go to other areas

 The full range of iCloud apps is displayed, including those for Pages, Numbers and Keynote

iCloud lets you sync emails, contacts, calendars and other items wirelessly (no need to physically plug the iPhone into the computer).

About the iCloud Drive

One of the options in the iCloud section is for the Cloud Drive. This can be used to store documents so that you can use them on any other Apple devices that you have, such as an iPhone or a MacBook. To set up iCloud Drive:

1 In the iCloud section of the Settings app, tap on the **iCloud Drive** button

☁ iCloud Drive   Off >

2 Tap on the **iCloud Drive** button so that it is **On**

❮ iCloud   iCloud Drive

iCloud Drive

Allow apps to store documents and data in iCloud.

Look Me Up By Email   >

3 Once iCloud Drive has been activated, tap on any listed apps so that they can use iCloud Drive

❮ iCloud   iCloud Drive

iCloud Drive

Allow apps to store documents and data in iCloud.

Look Me Up By Email   >

🖼 Keynote

📊 Numbers

✏ Pages

🧭 Safari

4 When you are using an app that has iCloud Drive capabilities it may ask you to turn on iCloud Drive for the specific app, if it has not already been done. Tap on the **OK** button and open the Settings app

Set Up iCloud
Go to Settings and select iCloud. Sign in and turn on iCloud Drive for Pages.

OK

5 In the Settings app, open the settings for the specific app (in this case, Pages) and drag the **Use iCloud** button to **On**. Any document created, or edited, by this app will automatically be stored in the iCloud Drive

‹ Settings **Pages**

ICLOUD

Use iCloud

6 The documents in the app on your iPhone can be viewed on your other Apple devices if you have iCloud turned on and iCloud Drive activated. For

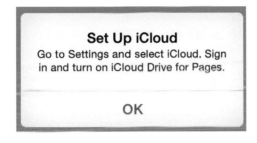

iOS 8 devices they can be viewed from the Documents section of the compatible apps (such as Pages, Numbers and Keynote); for OS X Yosemite devices they can be viewed in the iCloud Drive section in the Finder

Using iCloud Drive Online

Files that have been saved to your iCloud Drive on your iPhone can also be accessed on any other Apple devices you have, such as an iPhone or a MacBook. They can also be accessed from your online iCloud account at **www.icloud.com**, from any Internet-enabled computer. To do this:

 Log in to your iCloud account and click on the iCloud Drive button on the homepage

 Your iCloud Drive folders are displayed. Content created with the relevant apps on your iPhone will automatically be stored in the appropriate folders, i.e. Pages documents in the Pages folder, etc.

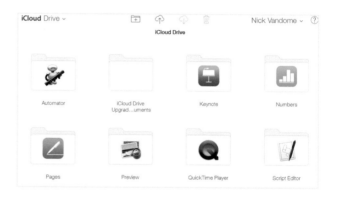

3 Click on a folder to view its contents. You can also edit documents or create new ones with the online iCloud. These changes will appear on your iPhone when the relevant apps are opened

Continuity and Handoff

One of the main themes of iOS 8 and the iPhone 6 is to make all of your content available on all of your Apple devices. This is known as continuity and handoff: when you create something on one device you can then pick it up and finish it on another device. This is done through iCloud. To do this:

 Ensure the app has iCloud turned on

 Create the content on the app on your iPhone

Open the same app on another Apple device, e.g. an iPad. The item created on your iPhone should be available to view and edit. Any changes will then show up on the file on your iPhone too

Continuing an email

Create an email on your iPhone and tap on **Cancel**

 Tap on **Save Draft**

Open the Mail app on another Apple device. The email will be available in the **Drafts** folder and can be continued here

About Family Sharing

As everyone gets more and more digital devices it is becoming increasingly important to be able to share content with other people, particularly family members. In iOS 8 the Family Sharing function enables you to share items that you have downloaded from the App Store, such as music and movies, with up to six other family members, as long as they have an Apple Account. Once this has been set up it is also possible to share items such as family calendars, photos and even see where family members are within Maps. To set up and start using Family Sharing:

1 Access the iCloud section within the Settings app, as shown on page 32

2 Tap on the **Set Up Family Sharing** button

3 Tap on the **Get Started** button

4 One person will be the organizer of Family Sharing, i.e. in charge of it, and if you set it up then it will be you. Tap on the **Continue** button (the Family Sharing account will then be linked to your Apple ID)

5 Tap on the **Continue** button again

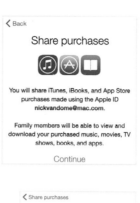

6 If you are the organizer of Family Sharing payments for items will be taken from the credit/debit card that you registered when you set up your Apple ID. Tap on the **Continue** button to confirm this

7 Once Family Sharing has been created, return to the iCloud section in the Settings app and tap on the **Add Family Member** button

8 Enter the name or email address of a family member and tap on the **Next** button

9 An invitation is sent to the selected person. They have to accept this before they can participate in Family Sharing

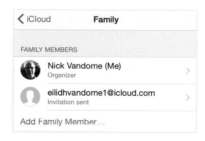

When you invite a family member you have an option for requiring them to ask for permission whenever they want to download anything from the App Store or the iTunes Store. This is usually done for children that are part of Family Sharing.

iCloud Photo Sharing
has to be turned On to
enable Family Sharing
(**Settings > Photos
& Camera > iCloud
Photo Sharing**).

When someone else
in your Family Sharing
circle adds a photo
to the Family album,
you are notified in the
Notification Center and
also by a red notification
on the Photos app.

Using Family Sharing

Once you have set up Family Sharing and added family members
you can start sharing a selection of items.

Sharing Photos

Photos can be shared with Family Sharing thanks to the Family
album that is created automatically within the Photos app. To use
this and share photos:

1 Tap on the **Photos** app

2 Tap the **Shared** button

3 The **Family** album is already
available in the **Shared** section.
Tap on the cloud button to access
the album and start adding photos
to it

4 Tap on this button
to add photos to the album

5 Tap on the photos
you want to add and
tap on the **Done**
button

6 Make sure the
Family album is
selected as the Shared
Album and tap on
the **Post** button

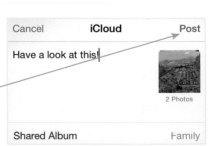

Finding family members

Family Sharing makes it easy to keep in touch with the rest of the family and see exactly where they are. This can be done with the Find My Friends app. The other person has to have their iPhone or iPad (or other Apple device) turned on and online. To find family members:

 Locate and download the **Find My Friends** app in the App Store

 Open the Find My Friends app to display all of the active family sharing devices. Tap once on a person's name to view their details and location. Tap on your own name and check that the **Share My Location** button is **On**

Me	Done
Great Britain	
Label My Location	Notifications
Share My Location	⬤

Sharing music, videos, apps and books

Family Sharing means that all members of the group can share purchases from the iTunes Store, the App Store or the iBooks store. To do this:

1 Open either **iTunes Store**, **App Store** or **iBooks**

2 Tap on the **Purchased** button (can be accessed from the **More** button)

℗ Purchased

3 Tap on a member of the Family Sharing group

FAMILY PURCHASES
Eilidh

4 The person's purchases are listed. Tap on a category to view those purchases and download them to your iPhone, if required

‹ Purchased	Eilidh	
♫	Music	›
⊞	Films	›
▭	TV Programmes	›

Beware

To use Find My Friends, all family members, or friends, have to have iOS 8 or OS X Yosemite installed as the operating system on their device. They also have to have shared their location, as in Step 2 here.

41

Hot tip

When Family Sharing is set up, a Family calendar is created in the Calendar app. This can be used to add events that can be seen by everyone in the Family Sharing group.

Camera

The iPhone 6 has a main, iSight, camera (back of phone) and a second camera on the front. The main camera is 8 megapixels (MP), and can shoot high resolution stills and HD video (1080p) up to 60 frames per second. The main camera also has a True Tone flash. The front VGA camera is used for FaceTime calls, and can takes photos and videos at 1.2 MP (photos) and HD video (720p).

Both photos and videos can be geotagged, so you can see where in the world you were when the photo or video was shot.

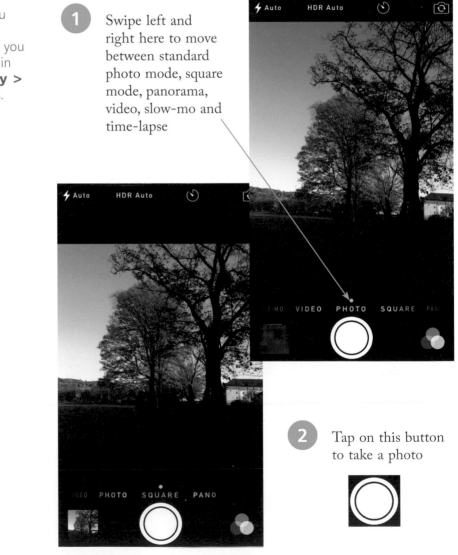

1 Swipe left and right here to move between standard photo mode, square mode, panorama, video, slow-mo and time-lapse

2 Tap on this button to take a photo

3 Tap on this button to toggle between the front- and back-facing cameras

Don't forget

The iPhone iSight camera has an improved autofocus system, improved face detection and image stabilization for improved clarity.

43

4 Tap on this button to select a filter effect to add to the photo you are going to take

Shooting video
Select the Video option as shown in Step 1 and you will see a Record button (red circle). Press to record video then press again to stop recording.

Searching with Spotlight

If you want to find things on your iPhone, there is a built-in search engine, Spotlight. This can search over numerous items on your iPhone and these can be selected within Settings:

Spotlight settings

Within the Settings app you can select which items the Spotlight search operates over. To do this:

Don't forget

To return to the Home screen from the Search page, tap once anywhere on the screen, or press the Home button.

 1 Tap on the **Settings** app

Hot tip

Enter the name of an app into the Spotlight search box and tap on the result to launch the app from here.

2 Tap on **General** tab

 General

3 Tap on the **Spotlight Search** link

 Spotlight Search >

4 Tap on an item to exclude it from the Spotlight search. Items with a tick will be included

< General **Spotlight Search**

SEARCH RESULTS

✓ Applications
✓ Spotlight Suggestions
✓ Contacts
✓ Music
✓ Podcasts
✓ Videos

Accessing Spotlight

The Spotlight search box can be accessed from any screen by pressing and swiping downwards on any free area of the Home screen. This also activates the keyboard. Enter the search keywords into the search box at the top of the window.

Don't forget

Spotlight can search over a range of areas, including nearby restaurants, movies and locations.

Searching with Siri

Siri is the iPhone voice assistant that provides answers to a variety of questions by looking at your iPhone and also web services. Initially, Siri can be set up within the **Settings** app:

1 In the **General** section, tap on the **Siri** link

Siri	>

2 Drag the **Siri** button to **On** to activate the Siri functionality. Tap on the links to select a language, set voice feedback and allow access to your details

Questioning Siri

Once you have set up Siri, you can start putting it to work with your queries. To do this:

1 Hold down the **Home** button until the Siri window appears

2 Ask a question such as, **Show me my calendar, Siri**

3 The results are displayed by Siri. Tap on an item to view its details. Tap on the microphone button to ask another question of Siri

Hot tip

You can ask Siri questions relating to the apps on your iPhone and also general questions, such as weather conditions around the world, or sports results. The results will be displayed by Siri or, if it does not know the answer, a web or Wikipedia link will be displayed instead.

Headphones

Apple supplies headphones that look a bit like iPod headphones. But there is a major difference: the iPhone headphones have a control on the right earpiece cable. This control houses the microphone needed for phone conversations when the headphones are plugged in. The control also allows the audio volume to be adjusted to make it louder or quieter.

By clicking the control, audio will pause. Two clicks in quick succession will skip to the next track.

The iPhone headphones are highly sophisticated and can be used to make calls, and divert callers to voicemail.

The iPhone supports a number of audio and video formats. The iPhone supports audio formats including AAC, Protected AAC, MP3, MP3 VBF, Audible (formats 2, 3, and 4), Apple Lossless, AIFF and WAV. In terms of video, the iPhone supports formats including .m4v, .mp4, Motion JPEG and .mov file formats.

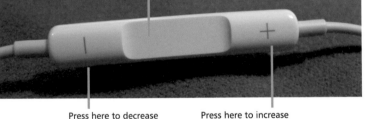

Press here ONCE to pause audio or answer call (press again at end of call)

To decline call press and hold for ~2 seconds

To switch to incoming or on-hold call, press once

Press here TWICE to skip to next track

To use Voice Control, press and hold

(this tiny control unit also contains the microphone!)

Press here to decrease volume

Press here to increase volume

Uses for the headphones – this is pretty obvious but consider

- Listening to music, podcasts, audio books

- Listening to the radio

- Watching movies

- Making phone calls

- Dictating VoiceMemos

- Giving Voice commands to your iPhone

Customizing the iPhone

Applications
The iPhone comes with many apps preinstalled by Apple. These can be moved around, or even placed on a different screen, but you cannot delete them from the iPhone. These apps are the core features of the iPhone.

The App Store has thousands of apps which we will look at later. Many are free while others are available for purchase. With so many apps available for download the chances are that there will be an app for most things you might want to do.

Ringtones
Apple has supplied several but people will always want to have their own unique ringtone. You can buy these from the App Store or make your own using iTunes or GarageBand. You can assign a specific ringtone to someone in your Contacts list so you know it's them calling when the phone rings.

Backgrounds and wallpapers
Again, there are several to choose from but you can make your own (use one of your photos) or you can download from third party suppliers. Try browsing the Internet for wallpapers or use a specific app.

Accessorizing the iPhone
You can use a screen protector to prevent scratches on the screen. There are many iPhone cases available. These are mainly plastic but leather cases are available as well. Placing your iPhone in a case or cover helps prevent marks or scratches on the phone.

Headphones
If you want to use headphones other than those provided by Apple, that's fine. You may get better sound from your music but you will not have the inbuilt microphone, which is very useful when you make a phone call.

USB to Lightning charger cable
With extensive use the iPhone battery may not last the whole day so you will probably need to carry around a spare charging cable. The USB to Lightning cable means you can plug it in to your PC or Mac at work and charge your iPhone during the day.

GarageBand is Apple's music-making app and it can be downloaded from the App Store.

Bluetooth drains power on your iPhone. Try to switch it off if you don't need it.

User Settings

There are many settings you can adjust in order to set the iPhone up to work the way you want. These will be discussed in detail later but they are shown briefly here.

As well as the settings already on the iPhone, many apps will have panels for their settings. If an app is not working the way you want, have a look under the Settings Control Panel and scroll to the bottom to see if your app has installed a settings panel.

The Wi-Fi Settings are grouped together with those for **Airplane Mode**, **Bluetooth**, **Cellular** and **Carrier**. Bluetooth can be used to scan for other compatible devices, which then have to be paired with the iPhone so that they can share content wirelessly.

Wi-Fi

Keep this off if you want to conserve power. Switching it on will let you join wireless networks if they are open or if you have the password.

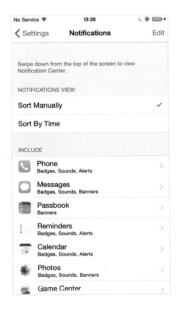

If a Settings option has an On/Off button next to it, this can be changed by swiping the button to either the left or right. Green indicates that the option is **On**.

Notifications

This is where you can set what items appear in the Notification Center, which is accessed by swiping down from the top of the screen.

Control Center

This is a set of shortcuts for regularly used items. See pages 28-29 for details.

Do Not Disturb

Use this to specify times when you do not receive alerts or FaceTime video calls.

General

This contains the largest range of settings, that can be used to check the software version on your iPhone, search settings, accessibility, battery usage and storage, date and time, keyboard settings and resetting your iPhone.

Display & Brightness

This can be used for adjusting the screen brightness, the display viewing size and using larger text sizes, or bold text.

Hot tip

The screen brightness can also be adjusted from the Control Center.

Wallpaper

Wallpaper is what you see when you press the Home button when the iPhone is locked. Use your own images or download from third party suppliers.

...cont'd

Hot tip

You can assign specific ringtones to selected contacts.

Beware

Your data on the iPhone is easily accessible if your iPhone is stolen. Use Touch ID & Passcode Lock and turn **Erase Data** On to wipe phone after 10 failed attempts.

Hot tip

One of the iCloud functions is the iCloud Keychain **(Settings > iCloud > Keychain)**. If this is enabled, it can keep all of your passwords and credit card information up-to-date across multiple devices and remember them when you use them on websites. The information is encrypted and controlled through your Apple ID.

Sounds

You can place the phone on vibrate or have the ringtone on. You can assign different tones for different contacts.

Touch ID & Passcode

This can be used to set up fingerprint security for unlocking your iPhone and also a numerical passcode (see page 53 for more details).

iCloud

This is where you can specify the items that are shared with the online iCloud service. This includes On/Off options for apps such as Notes and Calendars, and additional options for the Photos app.

Privacy

This contains a number of privacy options, including activating **Location Services**, so that apps such as Maps and Siri can use your location, using GPS. Location Services also has to be turned On if you want to use the **Find My iPhone** feature.

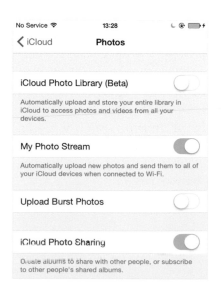

iTunes & App Store

This can be used to specify settings for
the online iTunes and App Store, such
as enabling automatic downloads when
there are updates to your existing apps or
music.

Mail, Contacts, Calendars

Use this for setting up new email
accounts and also specifying settings
for your existing accounts.

Apps' Settings

A lot of apps have their own settings,
including the pre-installed ones. Tap
on an app's name in the Settings app
to view its own specific settings. It
is worth checking Settings after you
install an app to see if it has installed a
settings file, since it may contain useful
features to help you set it up exactly
the way you want.

Using the Lock Screen

To save power, it is possible to set your iPhone screen to auto-lock. This is the equivalent of the sleep option on a traditional computer. To do this:

1   Tap on the **Settings** app

Settings

2   Tap on the **General** tab

General

3   Tap on the **Auto-Lock** link

Auto-Lock   1 Minute >

4   Tap on the time of non-use after which you wish the screen to be locked

< General   **Auto-Lock**

1 Minute

2 Minutes

3 Minutes   ✓

4 Minutes

5 Minutes

Never

5   Once the screen is locked, swipe here to the right to unlock the screen

No Service

13:43

Monday 22 September

slide to unlock

Touch ID

Fingerprint sensor

The iPhone 6 has a fingerprint sensor that can be used to unlock your iPhone. This is done by pressing your thumb or finger on the sensor to create a unique fingerprint code. To set this up:

1 Select **Settings > Touch ID & Passcode**

| | Touch ID & Passcode | > |

2 A passcode is required before Touch ID can be activated. Tap on the **Turn Passcode On** link

3 Enter a four-digit passcode

4 Tap on the **Add a Fingerprint** link. This presents a screen for creating your Touch ID. Place your finger on the Home button several times until the Touch ID is created. Use this to unlock your iPhone at the Lock Screen

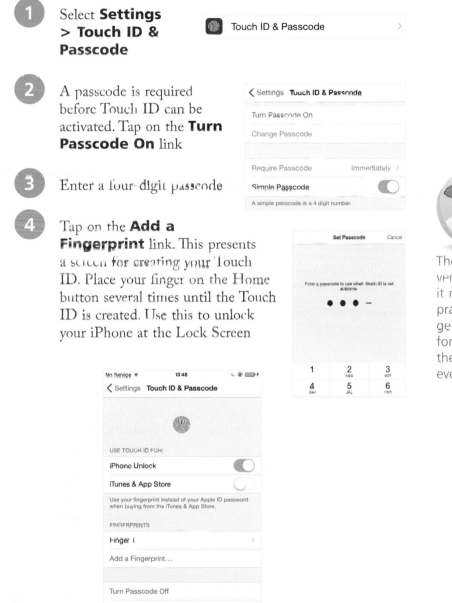

Don't forget

The fingerprint sensor is very effective, although it may take a bit of practise until you can get the right position for your finger to unlock the iPhone, first time, everytime.

Syncing Your Data

Your iPhone can store several types of information:

- Calendar
- Email
- Contacts
- Music
- Photos
- Videos
- Podcasts
- Apps (applications, i.e. programs)
- Documents

With iCloud, items such as Calendars, Contacts and Reminders get synced automatically once it has been set up. With iTunes on a computer you can sync items such as Music, Movies, TV Shows, Podcasts and iBooks. You will need to choose which media files and apps get synced when you plug your iPhone into your computer. You can also select to have iTunes sync your content automatically or do it manually for more control:

- You can opt *not* to open iTunes automatically when you plug the iPhone in.

- You can also choose to sync some types of content *manually* rather than automatically. To do this, scroll down to the bottom of the Summary window, when your iPhone is connected to iTunes on a computer, and check on the **Manually manage music and videos** button.

iTunes is the Apple music player that can also be used to download content from the online iTunes Store. It can also be used to download content directly onto an iPhone and also synchronize it from another computer.

When you connect your iPhone to your computer it will show up with this icon on the top toolbar.

Options

☐ Automatically sync when this iPhone is connected
☐ Sync with this iPhone over Wi-Fi
☐ Sync only checked songs and videos
☐ Prefer standard definition videos
☐ Convert higher bit rate songs to 128 kbps ⬍ AAC
☑ Manually manage music and videos
  [Reset Warnings]
  [Configure Accessibility...]

...cont'd

To sync your data with iTunes on a Mac or Windows PC:

 Connect your iPhone to the computer with the lightning USB connector. Click on the **Continue** button

Tap on the **Get Started** button in the next window. The categories on your iPhone are shown in the left-hand panel, including a Summary option

Hot tip

Automated syncs take the guesswork out of syncing.

Select a category to sync from the left-hand panel, e.g. Music, Movies or TV Shows and select the options for how you want the items synced

Tap on the **Apply** button to sync the selected items to your iPhone

Apply

Backup and Restore

Like any electronic device it is important to back up the content on your iPhone. This means that if something goes wrong with it then you will be able to restore the content from the backup. This can be done through iTunes on either a Mac or Windows PC. The backup can be also be sent to iCloud so that your content is stored there.

To back up your iPhone

The backup process can be performed using iTunes on either a Mac or Windows PC:

 Connect your iPhone to the computer with the lightning USB connector and click on it on the top toolbar. Click on the **Summary** tab

 Select how you would like the backup to be performed, i.e. with iCloud or on the computer to which your iPhone is connected

Backups

Automatically Back Up

⦿ iCloud
Back up the most important data on your iPhone to iCloud.

◯ This computer
A full backup of your iPhone will be stored on this computer.

☐ Encrypt iPhone backup
This will also back up account passwords used on this iPhone.

Change Password...

3 Tap on the **Back Up Now** button

Manually Back Up and Restore

Manually back up your iPhone to this computer or restore a backup stored on this computer.

Back Up Now   Restore Backup...

Latest Backup:
Today 11:47 to iCloud

4 The progress of the backup is displayed at the top of the iTunes window

Backing up "Nick's iPhone"... ✕

...cont'd

To restore the iPhone from a backup

If something does go wrong with your iPhone you can restore it to the latest backed up version. To do this:

1 Connect your iPhone to the computer with the lightning USB connector and click on it on the top toolbar. Click on the **Summary** tab

2 In the Summary window, click on the **Restore Backup** button

3 If you have made more than one backup you will be able to select which one you want to restore your iPhone with (the most recent one is usually the best option). Tap on the **Restore** button

Restore From Backup

Choose a backup to restore. This will restore only the contacts, calendars, notes, text messages, and settings, not the iPhone firmware.

iPhone Name: Nick's iPhone

Last Backed Up: Today 20:33

Cancel   Restore

4 The progress of the restore process is shown by this window and a similar message will display on your iPhone's screen

iPhone

Restoring iPhone from backup...

Time remaining: Less than a minute

Hot tip

Unlike an iPod, where you have to eject it from the PC or Mac before unplugging, you don't have to eject the iPhone – simply unplug it.

57

Data Roaming

Most of us travel abroad for business or pleasure. We like to take our cell phones to keep in touch with friends, family and the office. Call charges are much higher from overseas, and if you want to receive data (email, browse the web, and other activities) you will need to switch on Data Roaming.

Switch on Data Roaming

1 Go to **Settings > Cellular** (or **Mobile**)

2 Switch **Data Roaming** On if required

3 Switch Off when not needed

But beware – the cost of receiving data is very high and will be added to your phone bill. Your data package with your network supplier (e.g. AT&T, O2 etc.) will not cover the cost of downloading data using foreign networks!

Beware

Data Roaming allows you to receive data when away from your home country, but can be very expensive.

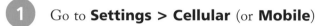

No Service 📶　　　14:35　　　🔋⚡

‹ Settings　　**Cellular**

Cellular Data 　　　　⬤

Enable 4G 　　　　　⬤

Turn off cellular data to restrict all data to Wi-Fi, including email, web browsing, and push notifications. Using 4G loads data faster.

Data Roaming 　　　　◯

EU Internet 　　　　　◯

Turn off data roaming when traveling to avoid charges when web browsing and using email, MMS, and other data services. EU Internet service only applies to Internet and personal hotspot data traffic.

Cellular Data Network 　　›

Personal Hotspot 　　　✳

CALL TIME

2 The Phone Functions

In this chapter we will look at how to use the phone functions to make and receive calls, maintain contact lists and make video calls using FaceTime.

Answering Calls

When you receive a call the iPhone will either ring or vibrate, depending on your iPhone settings. If the iPhone is locked, you will see the name of the caller on the screen and you will need to tap on the **Accept** button. If the iPhone is unlocked when the call comes in, you will be given the option to **Accept** or **Decline** (and send to voicemail).

When you receive an incoming call, you can answer by tapping on the green **Accept** button.

If you do not want to take the call and let it go to voicemail, tap on **Decline** or tap on the **Remind Me** button to be sent a reminder about the missed call at a certain time.

Tap on the **Message** button to send a text message to the person phoning.

Don't forget

After answering a call the options on the home screen include: muting the call; accessing the phone's keypad; putting the call on speaker; adding another call; making a video FaceTime call to the person; and adding the caller to your contacts.

After answering a call you will see the various options available.

Tap on the red button to end a call.

Making Calls Using Keypad

Although you can do a multitude of things with the iPhone, one of its basic functions is making phone calls. To do this:

 Tap on the **Phone** app

 Select the keypad icon. This brings up a standard keypad on the touch screen

 Dial the number. This appears at the top of the screen as you add it

Make FaceTime Video Calls

To use FaceTime

● The caller and recipient must both use iPhone 4 or later

● Alternatively, you can use a FaceTime-enabled Mac

● FaceTime calls can be made using Wi-Fi or Cellular

The FaceTime settings

Don't forget

FaceTime also has to be turned **On** in the **FaceTime** section of the **Settings** app.

1 Tap on the FaceTime app

2 Tap on this button to select a contact

3 Select a contact to call. This will be from the Contacts app

Don't forget

You can also make a FaceTime call to someone by selecting them in the **Contacts** app and tapping the FaceTime icon.

4 For the selected contact, tap on this button to make the FaceTime call

While the call is being accepted your own image appears in the main window

6 Recipient must tap **Accept**

If you have already had a FaceTime video call with someone you can go to **Recents** and make another FaceTime call.

 Once the call has been connected the recipient's image appears in the main window

Actions during a FaceTime call

1 Tap on this button to mute the call. You will still be able to see the caller

2 Tap on this button to toggle between the front and back cameras

3 Tap on this button to end a FaceTime call

Using the Contacts List

The Contacts app acts like your own address book on the iPhone:

 Tap the **Contacts** app on the Home screen

 Flick up or down until you find the contact you wish to call

Groups	All Contacts	+
	Q Search	
V		
Robin **V**		
Eilidh **Vandome**		
Lucy **Vandome**		
Mark **Vandome**		
Mike **Vandome**		

 Select the action you wish to take, e.g. send text message, phone the contact

No Service 🗐	14:46	📞 100% ▭ +
❮ All Contacts		Edit

Eilidh Vandome

mobile

FaceTime

home
eilidhvandome

iCloud
eilidhvandome

other
eilidhvandome

Game Center
{ Nick729 }

Notes

Send Message

Don't forget

The add photo function can also be used to edit an existing photo, or delete it.

Add photo to contact

If you want to assign a photo to a contact, access the contact, tap **Edit** and tap **Add Photo** next to their name. Select a photo or take a new one. This gives a more personalized phone call, instead of just seeing a name or a number on the screen.

Take Photo
Choose Photo
Edit Photo
Delete Photo
Cancel

Using the Favorites List

People you call regularly can be added to your favorites list. This is the first icon (from the left) when you open the phone application.

To add someone to your favorites list

 Open **Contacts**

 Select the contact you wish to add

3 Tap **Add to Favorites**

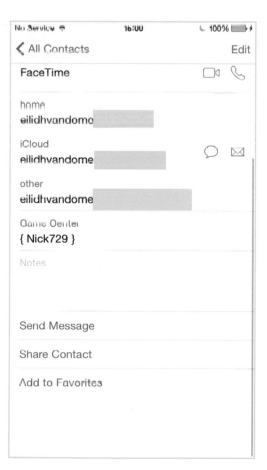

Add the contacts you call most to your Favorites List.

Recents List

Recent calls you have made or missed are listed under Recents.

Missed calls

● These are in the **Missed** tab and are listed in red

● **All** shows the calls made, received and missed

● Calls made are shown by the icon

● Calls received are shown without an icon

To return a call using Recents list

From the names shown in the Recents list, simply tap the name of the person you wish to call.

Assigning Ringtones

The iPhone has a number of polyphonic ringtones built in, or you can buy more from iTunes or even make your own. You can have the default tone for every caller or you can assign a specific tone for a contact.

To assign a ringtone

 Tap on the **Phone** app

 Select a contact then click **Edit**

Click on the **Ringtone** link

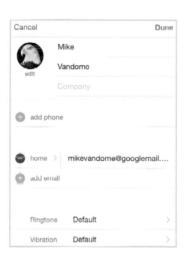

Choose the ringtone you wish to assign and tap on the **Done** button

Do Not Disturb

There are times when you do not want to see or hear Notifications from apps, or receive phone calls. For example, during the night you may want to divert all calls to voicemail rather than be woken up by phone calls.

 Open **Settings > Do Not Disturb**

 Slide the slider to **On** if you want to switch on Do Not Disturb

Allow some callers to get through

You may want to allow friends and family, or those in your favorites list to get through and not be diverted to voicemail.

 Open **Settings > Do Not Disturb**

 Choose the scheduled time (if you wish to schedule)

 Allow Calls From > choose **Everyone, No One, Favorites**, or specific groups

No Service 📶   15:16   🌙 100% 🔋⚡

‹ Settings   **Do Not Disturb**

Manual ⬤◯

When Do Not Disturb is enabled calls and alerts that arrive while locked will be silenced, and a moon icon will appear in the status bar.

Scheduled ◯

Allow Calls From   Favorites ›

Incoming calls from your favorites will not be silenced.

Repeated Calls ⬤◯

When enabled, a second call from the same person within three minutes will not be silenced.

SILENCE:

Always

Only while iPhone is locked   ✓

Incoming calls and notifications will be silenced while iPhone is locked.

Missed Calls

It happens to all of us from time to time: the boss calls and somehow you managed to miss it. If your iPhone was locked when he called, you can see at a glance that he has called.

You can find out exactly when he called by looking at the missed calls list.

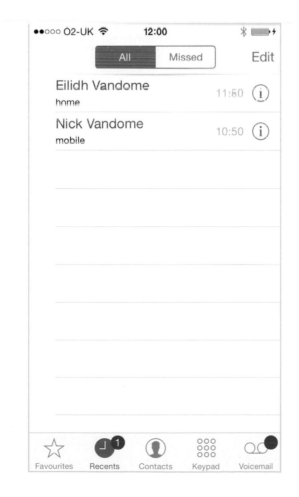

Make the Most of Contacts

The Contacts application on the iPhone lets you call someone, send them an SMS or MMS, email them, and assign them specific ringtones.

Add someone to Contacts

If you get a call from someone who is not in your contacts list, you can add them from the Phone app.

Try to enter as much contact information as possible, since this gives you more options for contacting them.

 Open the Phone app and tap on the **Recents** button on the bottom toolbar

 Recent calls and their numbers will be displayed

Select a number and tap on the **Create New Contact** button

 Enter the details for the contact and tap on the **Done** button. The contact's details will be added to the Contacts app

Adding Contacts

You can also add contacts directly into the Contacts app, so you can then access their details. To do this:

 Tap on the Contacts app

 Tap on the **+** button to add details for a new contact

Groups	All Contacts	+

Q Search

A

Tim and **Alison**

Jane **Allen**

Katriona **Allen**

Hotel **Ambasador**

Apple inc.

Apple **Inc.**

Stevie **Arnott**

Shafiq **Ashraf**

B

Peter **Badger**

Chris **Barron**

Mike **Barron**

3 Enter the details for the contact, including First and Last Name, Phone, Email and Address. Tap on the **Add Photo** button to browse to a photo, or take one with the camera. Tap on the green **+** buttons to include extra items for each field

Cancel	New Contact	Done

add photo — Steve

Last

Company

add phone

add email

Ringtone   Default   >

Vibration   Default   >

Text Tone   Default   >

Vibration   Default   >

4 Tap on the **Done** button. The contact's details will be added to the Contacts app

Deleting Contacts

It is relatively easy to delete contacts:

 Tap the contact you wish to remove

 Once their details are loaded tap **Edit** at the top right

No Service 🛜	15:26	🌙 100% ▭ ⚡
Cancel		Done

➕ add social profile

➕ add instant message

Notes

add field

LINKED CONTACTS

➕ link contacts...

Delete Contact

3 Scroll down to the bottom of the screen and tap **Delete Contact**

4 That's it!

Make Calls Using Headphones

You don't have to hold the iPhone to your ear each time you want to make a call. It is often more convenient to use the headphones. This means you can keep the phone on the desk and make notes during the call.

The headphones are very sophisticated – the right cord contains a white rectangular button which is useful when listening to music – but they are also great for making calls.

How to use the headphones

Make a phone call	Dial as normal and speak normally. You will hear the caller via the headphones and they will hear your voice, which is picked up by the inbuilt microphone
Answer a call	Click the middle of the control button once
Decline a call	Press the middle of the controller and hold for ~two seconds (you will hear two low beeps to confirm)
End call	Press the middle of the controller once
If already on a call and you wish to switch to an incoming call and put current call on hold	Press the middle button once to talk to Caller 2 (and press again to bring Caller 1 back)
Switch to incoming call and end the current call	Press and hold the middle of the controller for ~two seconds (you will hear two low beeps to confirm)
Use Voice Control to dial the number	Press and hold the middle button

You can use third party headphones with the iPhone but it is likely you will lose some functionality.

Hide or Show Your Caller ID

Sometimes you do not want the person you are calling to know your iPhone phone number. You can easily hide your number so it does not display on their screen.

1 Go to **Settings > Phone > Show My Caller ID**

‹ Settings	**Phone**
My Number	
Contact Photos in Favorites	⬤━
CALLS	
Respond with Text	›
Call Forwarding	›
Call Waiting	›
Show My Caller ID	›
Blocked	›
Dial Assist	⬤━

Dial assist automatically determines the correct international or local prefix when dialing.

2 Tap Show My Caller ID **On** or **Off** depending on whether or not you want it to show

‹ Phone	**Show My Caller ID**
Show My Caller ID	⬤━

Call Forwarding

Sometimes you need to forward calls from your iPhone to another phone. For example, if you are somewhere with no cell phone coverage. This is pretty straightforward.

Setting up call forwarding

1 Go to **Settings > Phone > Call Forwarding**

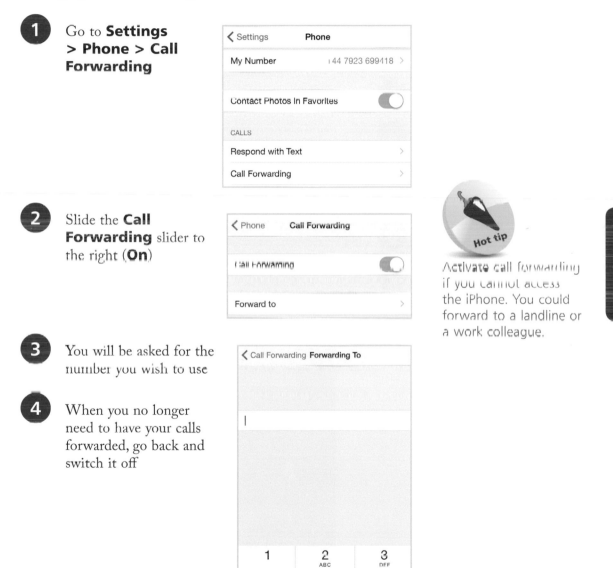

2 Slide the **Call Forwarding** slider to the right (**On**)

3 You will be asked for the number you wish to use

4 When you no longer need to have your calls forwarded, go back and switch it off

Hot tip

Activate call forwarding if you cannot access the iPhone. You could forward to a landline or a work colleague.

Conference Calls

This allows you to talk to more than one person at a time and is much like making conference calls using a landline.

Make a conference call

 Make a call

 Tap the **Add Call** icon on the screen

 The first call is put on hold

 Select another contact and make a call to them. Tap **Merge Calls**

 Tap **Merge Calls**

 Now everyone can hear each other

 Repeat until up to five people are on the same call

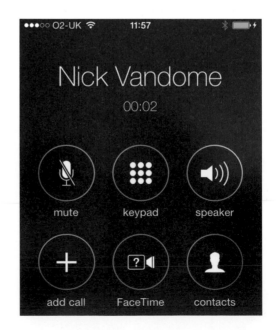

Visual Voicemail

This is a fantastic way to retrieve voicemail. No longer do you have to listen to irrelevant messages in order to hear the one you want. With Visual Voicemail you can tap the message you want to hear, and you can listen to that message and that message only.

To retrieve Visual Voicemail

1 Tap the **Phone** icon at the bottom of the screen

2 Tap the **Voicemail** icon at the far right

3 View the voicemail messages

4 Tap the one you want to hear

5 To listen again, tap the **Play** icon

6 If you want to listen to an earlier part of the message, **drag the progress slider to the left**

7 You can call the caller back by tapping **Call Back**

8 You can tap the arrow to the right of the message and add the caller to your Contacts list, or add them to the favorites list

What happens if Visual Voicemail is not available?
This sometimes happens but it's easy to get your voicemail:

1 Tap **Phone > Keypad**

2 Press and hold the **1** key

3 Retrieve your messages

Hot tip

Visual Voicemail makes it very easy to listen to specific voicemail messages.

Beware

Sometimes you cannot access Visual Voicemail (poor network signal). To retrieve your voicemails tap and hold "1" on the keypad.

Call Waiting

What is the value of call waiting? If call waiting is switched off, and someone phones you while you are on a call, they will be put straight through to voicemail. However, if call waiting is activated, they will know your line is busy and can wait until you are off the call. Or you can answer their call and put the first caller on hold.

 Go to **Settings > Phone**

 Tap **Call Waiting >**

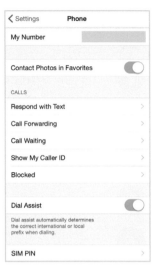

 Slide the **Off** button to the **On** position

iPhone Usage Data

How many SMS messages do you have left this month? Or talk minutes? There are times when you need to monitor your usage, since exceeding your limits on your contracted allowance will cost you extra.

How can you check how much you have used?
The iPhone has Usage data under **Settings > Cellular (Mobile)**. The information here is fairly limited in terms of what you have used, or have left, in this month's cycle.

Beware

If you exceed your monthly allowance on the iPhone you will be charged extra.

●●○○○ giffgaff 🛜	15:28	☾ 100% ▭▸⚡
‹ Settings	**Cellular**	

Personal Hotspot	Off ›

CALL TIME	
Current Period	3 Minutes
Lifetime	3 Minutes

CELLULAR DATA USAGE	
Current Period	306 KB
Current Period Roaming	0 bytes

USE CELLULAR DATA FOR:	
📹 FaceTime	⬤
✉️ Mail 39.3 KB	⬤
📔 Passbook	⬤
📈 Stocks 16.7 KB	⬤
☁️ Weather 19.1 KB	⬤

Third party applications
There are a number of apps that can track your monthly usage. These include *Optus Mobile Usage* for the US and *Allowance* for the UK. Other countries will have their own specific apps.

Third Party Apps for Usage

There are many apps for monitoring cellular and Wi-Fi data usage. One of these is Data Usage Monitor. Once you tell the app the billing data, it works out your usage for the month which will prevent you exceeding your data allowance. (If you are on unlimited data there's no need to worry!)

There are some great third party apps that help you monitor your monthly phone, text and data usage. Look for these in the App Store.

The app also comes with a useful built-in speed tester.

3 Messaging

Sending text and multimedia messages is no longer a chore. The iPhone carries out these functions effortlessly and this chapter shows how to use the Messages app for all of your messaging needs.

Text Messaging

Sending text messages on the iPhone 6 is a fast and efficient way to communicate using your iPhone. You can send messages as SMS (simple message system), MMS (multimedia message system – basically text with pictures), and iMessage.

SMS

You can send SMS, MMS and iMessages to multiple recipients. Simply add additional names in the **To** box when you create the message, as in Step 3.

SMS and MMS messages are sent over your mobile carrier's network. iMessages are sent to other Apple users with an Apple ID, using Wi-Fi.

Message settings can be specified in **Settings > Messages**. These include options for sending Read Receipts so that you are notified when someone reads your message.

1 Tap the **Messages** app on the Home screen

2 Tap the **New message** icon at the top right of the screen

3 Enter a recipient name or a phone number in the **To** box

4 Add any other names if you wish to send to more than one person

5 Go to the **text box** at the bottom and enter your message

6 Hit **Send**

7 The progress bar will show you the status of the message

8 Once sent, your message will appear in a green speech bubble (blue if iMessage)

9 Once the recipient replies, you will see their message below yours in a white speech bubble

iMessage

You can send iMessages using cellular or Wi-Fi to other people with iOS devices (or Macs). Simply send your text in the usual way. You will know it's an iMessage rather than SMS because your message will be in a blue speech bubble. You can also check the status of your text message (delivered or read) by checking below your message.

You can tell this message is an iMessage – you see iMessage at the top, plus my text is in a blue speech bubble. You can also see that my message was successfully delivered. If you see the **...** ellipsis in the speech bubble on the left, the person you texted is writing a reply.

Assign SMS messages a specific sound so you know you have received an SMS. This can be done in **Settings > Sounds > Text Tone** and select the sound you want to use.

To see how many characters you have used go to **Settings > Messages > Character Count > On**. 160 characters is the limit for one SMS.

Sometimes things go wrong, maybe you entered a wrong digit, and the message does not get sent, indicated by a red exclamation mark next to it. You can amend the number or tap on the red exclamation mark and tap on **Try Again**.

Using Predictive Text

Predictive text tries to guess what you are typing and also predict the next word following the one you have just typed. It is excellent for text messaging and it has now been introduced to the iPhone 6 with iOS 8. To use it:

1 Tap on the **General** tab in the Settings app

2 Tap on the **Keyboard** link

3 Drag the **Predictive** button **On**

4 When predictive text is activated the QuickType bar is displayed above the keyboard. Initially this has a suggestion for the first word to include. Tap on a word or start typing

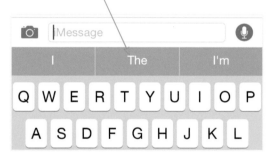

5 As you type, suggestions appear. Tap on one to accept it. Tap on the word within the quotation marks to accept exactly what you have typed

Predictive text learns from your writing style as you write and so gets more accurate at predicting words. It can also recognize a change in style for different apps, such as Mail and Messages.

6 If you continue typing, the predictive suggestions will change as you add more letters

7 After you have typed a word a suggestion for the next word appears. Tap on one of the suggestions, or start typing a new word, which will then also have predictive suggestions as you type

Toggling predictive text from the keyboard
You can also toggle predictive text On or Off from the keyboard. To do this:

1 Press on this button on the keyboard

2 Tap on the **Predictive** button to turn it **On** or **Off**

The button in Step 1 can also be used to add Emojis (or smileys) which are symbols used in text messages to signify happiness, surprise, sadness, etc.

Sending MMS Messages

The iPhone can send more than just plain boring text messages. MMS means Multimedia Message Service, which is basically a means of sending images, including video, to a recipient, rather than a simple SMS message. Each MMS counts as two SMS messages, so be careful how many you send.

To send an MMS

1 Tap **Messages** and tap the **New message** icon

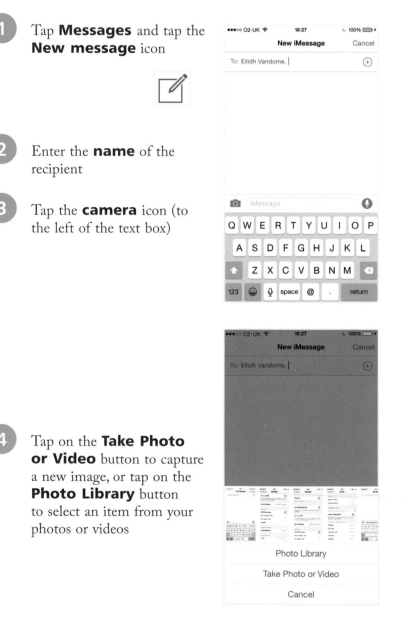

2 Enter the **name** of the recipient

3 Tap the **camera** icon (to the left of the text box)

4 Tap on the **Take Photo or Video** button to capture a new image, or tap on the **Photo Library** button to select an item from your photos or videos

5 Browse to the picture or video you want to send, from within the **Photos** app, and tap on the **Choose** button to select it

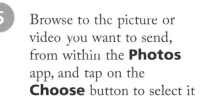

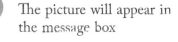

6 The picture will appear in the message box

7 Type your text message to accompany the picture or video

8 Hit **Send**

Sending Audio Clips

You can also send audio messages in an iMessage so that people can hear from you to. To do this:

1 Open a new iMessage

2 Press and hold on the microphone icon at the right-hand side of the text field

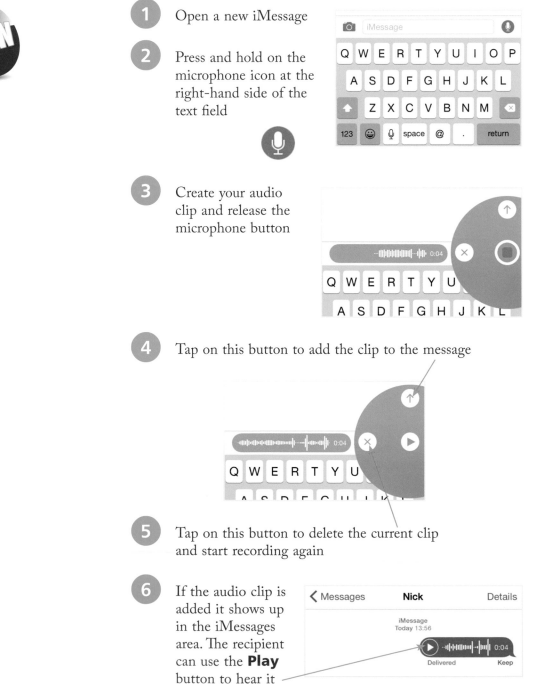

3 Create your audio clip and release the microphone button

4 Tap on this button to add the clip to the message

5 Tap on this button to delete the current clip and start recording again

6 If the audio clip is added it shows up in the iMessages area. The recipient can use the **Play** button to hear it

Sharing Your Location

With Messages you can now also show people your location (by sending a map) rather than just telling them. To do this:

1 Open conversation where someone has asked where you are, tap once on the **Details** button

2 Tap once on the **Details** button

3 Tap once on the **Send My Current Location**, or **Share My Location** buttons

4 For Share My Location, tap once on one of the options for how long you want your location to be shared for. These include sharing for an hour, a day or indefinitely

5 Your location is shown on a map and sent to the other person in the conversation

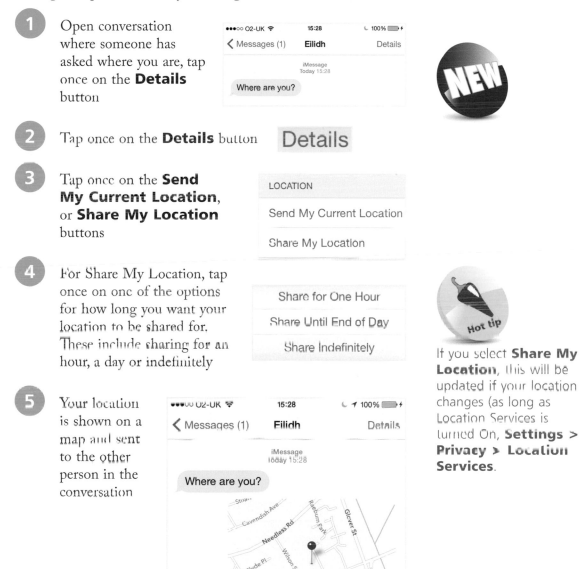

68

Hot tip

If you select **Share My Location**, this will be updated if your location changes (as long as Location Services is turned On, **Settings > Privacy > Location Services**.

Managing Text Messages

Forwarding a text message

You can easily forward a text message to another person.

1 Open the message and press and hold on the message

2 Tap on the **More** button

3 Tap on the **Forward** button and enter a recipient name

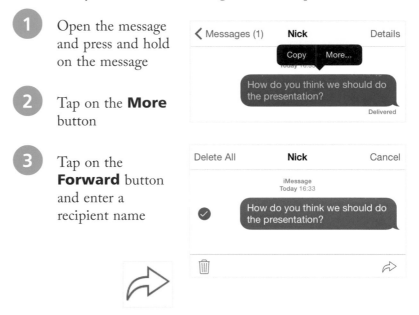

Deleting a text message

1 Open Messages to show your list of text messages

2 Swipe the text message left to right then tap **Delete**

In the App Store there are several apps that let you message friends and colleagues. Examples include Skype, WhatsApp, Viber, and others.

Editing text messages

You can selectively delete parts of a text message thread:

1. Open the message and press and hold on the message

2. Tap on the **More** button

3. Tap next to a message to select it

4. Tap on **Delete All** to delete the selected messages, or tap on the **Trash** icon

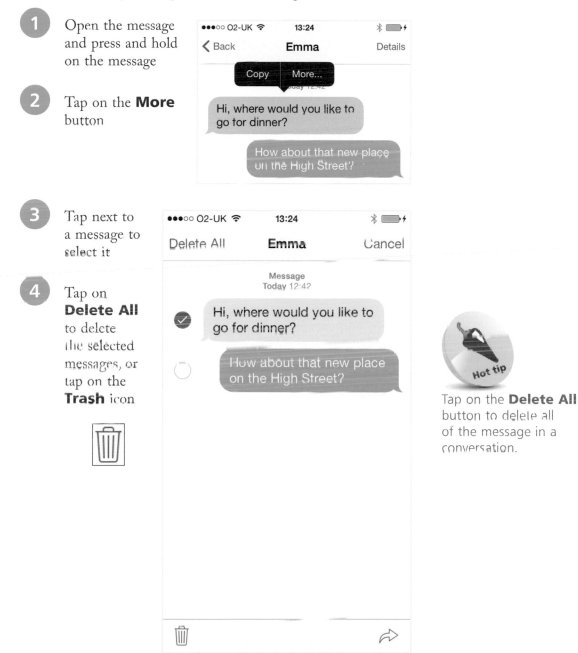

Tap on the **Delete All** button to delete all of the message in a conversation.

Live Links

When you send a text message, an email, or use a social networking app where text is inserted, you can add phone numbers, web URLs and email addresses. The recipient can then click on these to return the call, visit a website, or send an email.

SMS with telephone number
Tap on a phone number in a message to call it

URLs, email addresses and phone numbers in messages, web pages and emails are live and can be tapped to call the number, view other web pages or send emails.

SMS with email address

Tap on an email address in a message to create an email to that person

Live links to phone numbers and email addresses don't end with Mail. You can use phone numbers in Safari. If you see a number you want to dial on a web page, put your finger on the number and keep your finger there until a box pops up showing you the various options. These include calling the number, sending a text message, creating a new contact or adding to an existing contact.

Live links in emails
If you send an email to someone and include a website, email address or URL these are also clickable.

Click on the link to go to that site in a web browser.

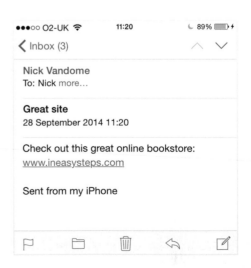

4 Music and Movies

The iPhone is a workhorse but is also a fun device, able to play music and movies with excellent sound quality and superb visual quality on the Retina HD screen. This chapter shows how to obtain, play and manage music on your iPhone and also view movies and other similar content from the iTunes Store.

The Music App

The music app can be used to turn your iPhone into your own personal jukebox. To use it:

 Tap on the **Music** app on the Dock

If you don't like the way the various functions are shown on the Music app you can change these. Go to **Settings > Music**.

 Browse for music using the bottom toolbar in the Music app

The Music app suggests songs and albums that it thinks go well together. These appear when you tap on the **Store** button from the Music app and tap on the **More** button The suggestions appear under **Genius** and get updated as you download more music.

 Tap on the **More** button to view more options, such as Composers

Play Audio on the Music App

The Music app is very versatile for playing your favorite albums and tracks. To use it:

 Tap on the **Music** app on the Dock

 Tap **Artists** if you want to search this way, or choose **Playlists** or **Songs**

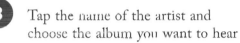 Tap the name of the artist and choose the album you want to hear

 Tap on the track that you want to play. If you select the first track of an album then the other tracks will play in sequence after it

 The selected track starts playing in the Music app interface

Hot tip

You can play a song from your music library by using Siri. Hold down the Home button until Siri appears and then say, 'Play, (name of song)' and it should start playing automatically.

Music App Controls

Once a track is playing in the Music app there are a number of controls that can be used.

 Tap once on the middle button to pause/play the currently-playing track. Use the buttons on either side to move to the beginning or end of a track

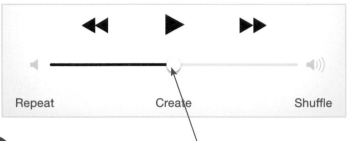

Repeat   Create   Shuffle

Hot tip

The volume can also be changed using the controls on the iPhone headphones (see page 46), or with the volume button on the side of the iPhone.

 Drag this button to increase or decrease the volume

 Tap once on this button to repeat a song or album after it has played

 **Repeat**

4 Tap once on this button to shuffle the order of songs on your iPhone

Shuffle

Cover View
In any view in the Music app, rotate your iPhone to landscape to view thumbnails of the albums on your phone.

Hot tip

Music controls, including Play, Fast Forward, Rewind and Volume can also be applied in the **Control Center**, which can be accessed by swiping up from the bottom of the screen.

View the Music Tracks

Sometimes you want to see what tracks are available while you are listening to audio.

While viewing the album artwork screen

 Tap the small **bullet list** icon at the top right of the screen

 The album cover flips to show audio tracks available

To get back to the main screen again, tap on the **Done** button at the top right

Search for Music

Sometimes you can't see the music or artist you are looking for. Hit the search tool at the top right of the Music app screen and type the name of the artist, album, song, podcast, or whatever you are looking for.

Hot tip

You can search for audio or video in your Music app within the Music app itself, or you can use Spotlight.

1 Tap on this bar to search for items in alphabetical order

2 Tap in the **Search** box and enter a song or artist. Tap on one of the results

Creating Your Own Playlists

Using the Music app you can create your own playlists.

To set up your own playlist

 Go to **Music > Playlists**

 Tap **New Playlist...**

3 Name it and tap on the **Save** button

4 Tap the **+** icon to add songs and tap on the **Done** button

5 If you want to remove or edit the playlist, open the playlist and tap **Edit**

When a track is playing, tap on the **Create** button to create a **Genius Playlist**. This is a playlist that is created automatically by the Music app, based on similar songs in your music library.

97

Buying Music

Music on the iPhone can be downloaded and played using the iTunes and the Music apps respectively. iTunes links to the iTunes Store, from where music, and other content, can be bought and downloaded to your iPhone. To do this:

 Tap once on **iTunes Store** app

 Tap once on the **Music** button on the iTunes toolbar at the bottom of the window

 Use the buttons at the bottom of the window to view the music content, or swipe up and down, and left and right in the main window

Beware

You need to have an Apple ID with credit or debit card details added to be able to buy music from the iTunes Store.

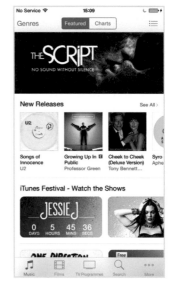

 Tap once on an item to view it. Tap once here to buy an album or tap on the button next to a song to buy that individual item

 Purchased items are included in the Music app's Library

Watching Movies

The iPhone is a great video player.

 Tap on the **Videos** app

 To find content, tap on the **Store** button

 Browse the video store to select a title and download it

4 Select the video in the **Videos** app and tap the **Play** button. The playback screen will automatically rotate to landscape

5 Adjust volume, rewind and other features using the controls which are shown below

6 If you want to stop, simply press the **Play/Pause** button and it will save your place

You can also watch YouTube videos on your iPhone, by either going to the YouTube website in Safari, or by downloading the YouTube app from the App Store.

You have a few ways of getting videos on your iPhone: home movies, either using a camcorder or the iPhone camera; convert your purchased DVDs to iPhone format; buy or rent movies from the iTunes store. DVDs can be converted with an app such as Handbrake, but make sure it is legal to do so.

Podcasts

The iPhone is also great for listening to audiobooks and podcasts. This can be done with the Podcasts app that can be downloaded from the App Store.

 Open the **Podcasts** app (which now comes preinstalled with iOS 8)

 Tap on the Podcasts app to open it and view the available podcasts (which can be audio and video)

 Tap on a podcast to download it to your iPhone

Tap on a podcast to listen to it. If a podcast has a red circle on it with a number, this means that there are updates available for it

5 Photos and Videos

The iPhone has two built-in cameras, and is able to shoot video as well as still images. In addition, you can manage and edit your photos and videos directly on the iPhone itself.

Sharing Content

Since the iPhone can store and create such a great range of content, it seems a shame to keep it all to yourself and there are options for sharing all kinds of content. The example here is for one of the most popular, sharing photos, but the process also applies to other content such as web pages, notes and contacts.

 Open a photo at full size and tap on the **Share** button

 Tap on one of the options for sharing the photo. These include messaging, emailing, sending to iCloud, adding to a contact in your Contacts app, using as your iPhone wallpaper, tweeting, sending to Facebook or Flickr, printing and copying the photo

 The photo is added to the item selected in Step 2, in this case an iMessage in the Message app

Sharing with AirDrop

AirDrop is a feature for sharing files wirelessly over short distances. It has been available on Mac computers for a number of years and it now comes to the iPhone 6. To use it:

 Swipe up from the bottom of the screen to open the Control Center, to activate AirDrop

 Tap on the **AirDrop** link

 Select how you want to share your files with other AirDrop users. This can be with your contacts in the Contacts app, or Everyone

You can make yourself discoverable to everyone or only people in your contacts.

Off

Contacts Only

Everyone

Cancel

Select an item you want to share, such as a photo in the Photos app, and tap on the **Share** button

If there are people nearby with AirDrop activated, the AirDrop button will be blue on your iPhone

AirDrop. Share with people nearby. If you don't see them, have them turn on AirDrop in Control Center on iOS, or go to AirDrop in Finder on a Mac.

Tap on an available icon to share your content with this person (they will have to accept it via AirDrop once it has been sent)

Tap to share with AirDrop

Nick

Beware

There have been some issues with AirDrop working properly on iOS devices. Make sure you are as close as possible to the other user and that they have AirDrop turned on in the Control Center. If it is a contact, make sure that you have their iCloud email in your Contacts app.

Where Are My Pictures?

As shown in Chapter One, the iSight camera can be used to capture photos and video. Once these have been captured they can be viewed and organized in the Photos app. To do this:

1 Tap on the **Photos** app

2 At the top level, all photos are displayed according to the years in which they were taken

3 Tap within the **Years** window to view photos according to specific, more defined, timescales. This is the **Collections** level. Tap on the **Years** button to move back up one level

4 Tap within the **Collections** window to drill down further into the photos, within the **Moments** window. Tap on the **Collections** button to go back up one level

Moments are created according to the time at which the photos were added or taken: photos added at the same time will be displayed within the same Moment.

5 Tap on a photo within the **Moments** window to view it at full size. Tap on the **Moments** button to go back up one level

Double-tap with one finger on an individual photo to zoom in on it. Double-tap with one finger again to zoom back out. To zoom in to a greater degree, swipe outwards with thumb and forefinger.

Creating Albums

Within the Photos app it is possible to create different albums in which you can store photos. This can be a good way to organize them according to different categories and headings. To do this:

1 Tap on the **Albums** button

2 Tap on this button

Albums

3 Enter a name for the new album

4 Tap on the **Save** button

New Album
Enter a name for this album.

Madeira

Cancel   Save

When photos are placed into albums the originals remain in the main **Photos** section.

5 Tap on the photos you want to include in the album

6 Tap on the **Done** button

Done

Add 5 photos to "Madeira".

< Collections   **Moments**   Done

16 November 2013   Select

12 March   Select

13 March   Deselect

7 Tap on the **Albums** button to view the album

Madeira
5

Photos   Shared   Albums

Selecting Photos

It is easy to take hundreds, or thousands, of digital photos and most of the time you will only want to use a selection of them. Within the Photos app it is possible to select individual photos so that you can share them, delete them or add them to albums.

 Access the Moments section and tap on **Select** button

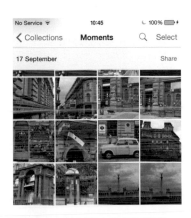

Press and hold on a photo to access an option to copy it, rather than selecting it.

2 Tap on the photos you want to select, or tap on the **Select** button again to select all of the photos

To add items to an album, tap on this button in the **Moments** section.

Select

Tap on photos to select them, then tap on the **Add To** button and select either an existing album or tap on the **New Album** link to create a new album with the selected photos added to it.

3 Tap on the **Deselect** button if you want to remove the selection

4 Use these buttons to, from left to right, share the selected photos, delete them or add them to an album

Editing Photos

The Photos app has options to perform some basic photo-editing operations. To use these:

1 Open a photo at full-screen size and tap once on the **Edit** button to access the editing tools Edit

2 Tap on the **Enhance** button to have auto-coloring editing applied to the photo

3 Tap on the **Crop** button and drag the resizing handles to select an area of the photo that you want to keep and discard the rest

4 Tap on the **Rotate** button to rotate the photo 90 degrees at a time, anti-clockwise

5 Tap on the **Filters** button to select special effects to be applied to the photo

6 Tap on the **Enhance** button to have auto-coloring editing applied to the photo

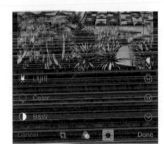

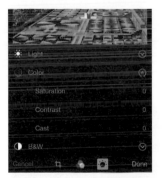

If you reopen a photo that has been edited and closed, you have an option to **Revert** to its original state, before it was edited.

7 For each function, tap on the **Done** button to save the photo with the selected changes

8 Tap on the **Cancel** button to quit the editing process

Taking Videos

To capture your own video footage:

1 Tap the **Camera** icon to load the app. The shutter will open to show the image

2 Drag just above the shutter button until **Video** is showing

3 Tap on the red **Record** button

Hot tip

Hold phone in landscape mode when shooting video.

Hot tip

Videos are located in the Photos section within the **Photos** app.

4 The **Record** button turns into a red square during filming

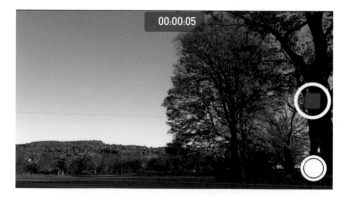

5 When you have finished, tap the Record button again. Your video will be in the Camera Roll Album

Editing the Video

You can edit the video you have taken on a Mac, PC or directly on the iPhone itself.

 Tap the **Photos** app

 Access the video in the same way as for accessing photos

 Tap the video to open it – the image can be viewed in portrait or landscape, but landscape is easier for trimming

 Touch the screen and the trimming timeline will be shown at the top of the screen

 Decide what (if anything) you want to trim and drag the sliders on the left and right until you have marked the areas you wish to trim

Video editing is now non-destructive which means you can trim your video, but the original video clip is left intact.

113

 Tap the blue **Trim** icon at the top right of the screen and the unwanted video will be removed

 Tap on the **Save as New Clip** button to save the edited clip

Save as New Clip

Cancel

Creative Shots

The iPhone camera can also be used to create a range of video effects: you can create panorama, slow-motion shots or time-lapse effects. To do this:

Panoramas

 For panoramas, open the **Camera** and select the **Pano** option by swiping along

 Once you tap the photo icon (bottom of screen) you need to **pan from left to right keeping the arrow on the center line** for best results

Move iPhone continuously when taking a Panorama.

 Once the arrow reaches the right side, the panoramic image will be created and saved in the Photos app (or tap this button to stop the panorama at that point)

Slow Motion

 For slow-motion, select the **Slo-Mo** option and tap on the shutter button

 The Slo-Mo option records video at 240 frames per second to create the slow motion effect

 Tap the shutter button again to stop recording

Time-lapse

 For time-lapse, select the **Time-lapse** option and tap on the shutter button

 The camera keeps taking photos periodically until you press the shutter button again

Time-lapse shots are created like videos, with each frame that has been captured being played in sequence.

6 The Standard Apps

Each iPhone comes preinstalled with a core set of applications (apps), which make it so versatile and useful. In this chapter we explore the apps that haven't been covered in other chapters and show how to get the best use out of them.

Calendar

For people who want to get organized, people in business, education and many other sectors, the core applications are: Calendar, Mail, Contacts, Phone and Notes.

These apps integrate well with each other on the iPhone and also the PC and Mac.

Setting up Calendar

Before you start entering data into Calendar, there are one or two settings you should check:

Make sure your Time Zone is set correctly or all your appointments will be incorrect.

Turn Calendars **On** in iCloud (**Settings > iCloud**) to ensure your calendar events are saved to iCloud and so will be available on other iCloud-enabled devices.

 Go to **Settings > Mail, Contacts, Calendars**

 Tap **Mail, Contacts, Calendars** to open

3 Scroll down the page until you find **Calendars**

 Tap **Time Zone Override** to override the automatic time zone

5 Choose what to **Sync** (Do you want all events or just those for the past two weeks, month, three months, or six months?)

6 Set your **Default Calendar** – when you make new appointments using Calendar this is where the appointments will be added

No Service 🗢	15:44	🔋⚡
‹ Settings Mail, Contacts, Calendars		
My Info		Nick Vandome >
Import SIM Contacts		
CALENDARS		
Time Zone Override		Off >
Alternate Calendars		Off >
Week Numbers		
Show Invitee Declines		
Sync		Events 1 Month Back >
Default Alert Times		>
Start Week On		>
Default Calendar		Home >
New events created outside of a specific calendar will default to this calendar.		

(You can add to another calendar quite easily, though.)

Calendar Views

To start using the Calendar:

1 Tap the **Calendar** icon to open the app

2 You will see the **Month View** – if it opens in **Day** or **List**, tap on the **Month** name at the top of the screen

3 This shows an overview of the month

4 A gray dot means you have an appointment on that day, but it does not tell you how long the appointment is or what it is. But tap on the dot and you will see what the day's appointments are

5 If you need a detailed view of your appointments, check out the **Day** view (see next page)

Back to year view

Today

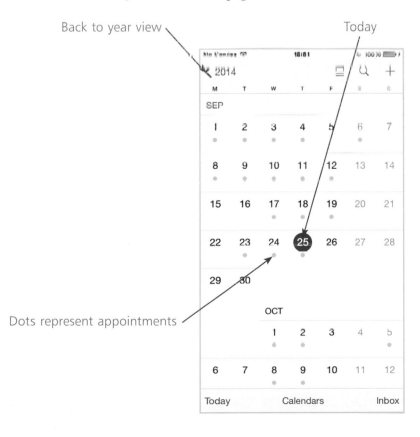

Dots represent appointments

Hot tip

The Calendar uses continuous scrolling to move through Month view. This means you can view weeks across different months, rather than just viewing each month in its entirety, i.e. you can view the second half of one month and the first half of the next one in the same calendar window.

Hot tip

Tap on the **Today** button to view the calendar for the current day. From Day view, tap on the month button in the top left-hand corner to go to Month view. Tap on a date within the month to view it, with the days for the corresponding week at the top of the window. Swipe left and right on this to move between different weeks.

...cont'd

6 Tap on the **Today** button to view the calendar for the current day (tap on the red dot in Month view to go to that day). From Day view, tap on the month button in the top left-hand corner to go to Month view

To add more calendars, tap on the **Calendars** button and then the **Edit** button. Tap on the **Add Calendar** button at the bottom of the window and enter the required details.

7 Tap on a date within the month to view it, with the days for the corresponding week at the top of the window. Swipe left and right on this to move between different weeks

8 Tap on the **Calendars** button at the bottom of the window to view the available calendars

Calendars

9 Tap on the **Inbox** button to view any invitation that you have been sent

10 Tap on the **List** button to view a scrollable list of all of your events

Searching Calendar

It's very easy to find appointments using the Search function within Calendar. You can also use Spotlight Search to find appointments.

 Tap **Calendar** to open

 Tap on the **List** button

 Tap the **Search box** for an item, e.g. Blue. After you enter a few letters the appointments containing those letters will appear below

 Tap a found appointment to see its details

You can search your calendar using the inbuilt search tool or use Spotlight.

Spotlight Search

You can also search for appointments using the iPhone Spotlight Search. To do this:

1 Swipe downwards anywhere on the Home screen to access the Spotlight Search

2 Enter a search word or phrase. This will search over all of the content on your iPhone, including within Calendars

3 Tap on one of the entries under the **Events** heading in the search results

Adding Appointments

Set up new appointment

To create a new appointment, or event, in the Calendar app:

 Tap on this button to create a new event or press and hold on a time slot

 Enter a Title and a Location for the event

Drag the **All-day** button to Off to set a timescale for the event

 Tap on the **Starts** button and drag on the barrels to set the time at which the appointment will start

 Do the same for the **Ends** time for the appointment

6 Tap on the **Alert** button and select a time at which you want an alert about the appointment

No Service	09:13	
‹ New Event	**Event Alert**	

None

At time of event

5 minutes before

15 minutes before

30 minutes before

1 hour before

2 hours before

1 day before

2 days before

1 week before

7 Tap on the **Calendar** button and select a calendar on which you would like the appointment to be included

No Service	00:14	
‹ New Event	**Calendar**	

• Home ✓

• Work

• Birthdays

• Family
  Shared with Eilidh Vandome

8 Tap on the **Repeat** button and select a time for when you want the appointment or event to be repeated. This is a good option for items such as birthdays

No Service	09:14	
‹ New Event	**Repeat**	

✓ Never

Every Day

Every Week

Every 2 Weeks

Every Month

Every Year

Custom ›

Set up your repeat items, such as birthdays and anniversaries.

121

Notes App

All good smartphones have some kind of note-taking software and the iPhone is no exception. The Notes apps is excellent for jotting down your thoughts and ideas:

To make a note

1 Tap the **Notes** icon to open the app

2 All of your notes will be displayed. Tap on one to access it and edit it

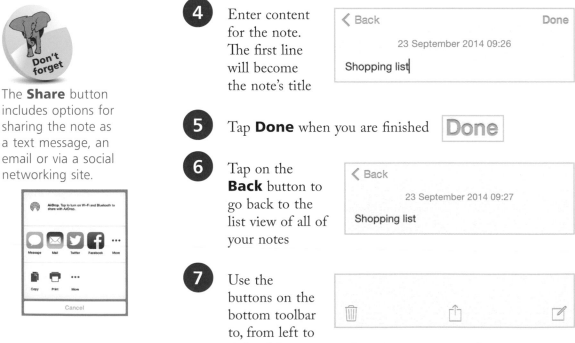

No Service	09:26	
‹ Folders		New
iPad iOS 8	Saturday ›	
iPad Seniors iOS 8	Thursday ›	
Menus	Tuesday ›	
New Note	Tuesday ›	
iPhone 6 Standard	08/09/2014 ›	
Things to pack	01/09/2014 ›	
Budget	29/08/2014 ›	
iPhone 6 Seniors	20/08/2014 ›	

3 Tap the **New** button to make a new note

New

4 Enter content for the note. The first line will become the note's title

‹ Back   Done
23 September 2014 09:26
Shopping list

5 Tap **Done** when you are finished   Done

6 Tap on the **Back** button to go back to the list view of all of your notes

‹ Back
23 September 2014 09:27
Shopping list

7 Use the buttons on the bottom toolbar to, from left to right, delete a note, share it or create another new note

Reminders

iOS 8 includes Reminders, a simple to-do list app that be used to save details about important events, meetings or simply items of shopping to buy. Reminders can be stored in the iCloud.

Using Reminders

 Tap **Reminders** to open the app

 Tap on a list to add a reminder to it, or tap the **New List** button to create a new list

 The keyboard will appear. Type the name of your reminder

Tap the **i** button if you want to add more details

Location-based Reminders

You can ask Reminders to alert you when you are leaving or arriving at a location. For example, you might want to pick up your dry cleaning when you are near that location. By entering the zip code, Reminders will know where you are and if you are near the dry cleaners it will remind you to pick up your dry cleaning.

Maps App

Maps is a great application – it can help you find where you are now, where you want to go, help you plan the route, tell you which direction you are facing and where all the traffic is.

124

Don't forget

Maps will only work with its full functionality if Location Services is switched On.

Hot tip

To see which way you are facing, tap the search icon (bottom left) until it shows a blue beam.

Hot tip

Satellite view can also be used for the Flyover feature, or Flyover Tour, if this is available for the selected area.

Open maps, you are here

Tap the blue circle to view details

Press and hold to drop a pin

Satellite 3D view

Hybrid view

Finding a route

Tap the Directions button and enter your start and end points.

Maps will calculate a route. It will also tell you how long it will take by car, public transport and by foot.

 By default, your current direction is used for the **Start** field. If you want to change this, tap and enter a new location or address

 Enter a destination (**End**) location or address

 Tap on the **Route** button on the keyboard (or at the top of the Directions window)

4 The route is shown on the map

5 Tap on the **Start** button to get directions

6 The route is shown on the map with directions for each section. As you follow the directions they will change for the next step of the journey

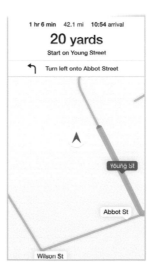

Hot tip

The Google Maps app is a good alternative that can be downloaded to your iPhone 6. It includes voice-guided, turn-by-turn navigation, live traffic conditions and information on public transport. Google claims to constantly keep the "map of the world" updated!

iBooks

The iBooks app was not previously a preinstalled app on earlier versions of the iPhone. However, it comes preinstalled with iOS 8 and can be used to download and read books on your iPhone.

Tap on it to view your library

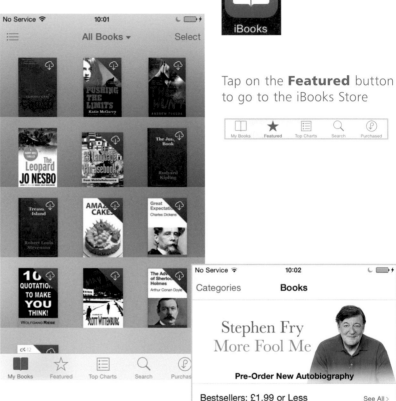

Hot tip

Newsstand is very similar to iBooks, but can be used to download and read magazines and newspapers instead of books.

Tap on the **Featured** button to go to the iBooks Store

View, preview and download new books to read on your iPhone. These will be placed in the iBooks Library (above)

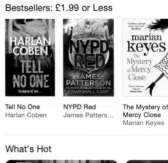

Game Center

For all gaming fans, this app can be used to download and play games from the App Store and also play against other people in multi-player games and compare your scores and achievements with other players.

 Tap on the Game Center app to view your own gaming details. You have to log in with your Apple ID to use Game Center and all of its features

 Use the bottom toolbar to access games and also add friends so that you can compete against them and compare scores

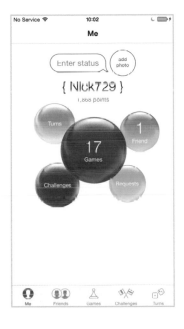

 Tap on the **Games** button to view the games that you have within Game Center and also download more from the App Store

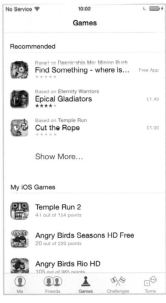

Health

The new Health app in iOS 8 is designed to collect a range of health and fitness information, such as body measurements, nutrition, fitness and sleep. It can also be used in conjunction with other health and fitness apps from the App Store and aggregate information from these too. To use the Health app:

 Tap on the this icon on the Home screen

 Use the buttons at the bottom of the screen to access the different sections

 Tap on the **Health Data** button to view the available categories

4 Tap on a category to view the options. Tap on an item on each page to select it and then fill in the data as required

Tap on the **Add Data Point** button within a category of the Health Data section to add the data for that item.

5 Tap on the **Dashboard** button to view the collated information from items that you have completed in the Health Data section

Dashboard

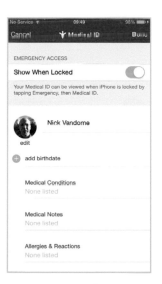

Beware

If you are concerned about any medical condition, always seek medical advice from your own doctor.

129

6 Tap on the **Sources** button to view any apps that are accessing the Health app

Sources

7 Tap on the **Medical ID** button to add any important medical information such as medical condition, blood type and allergies

Medical ID

Notification Center

Although the Notification Center feature is not an app in its own right, it can be used to display information from a variety of apps. These appear as a list for all of the items you want to be reminded about or be made aware of. Notifications are set up within the Settings app. To do this:

1 Tap on the **Settings** app

2 Tap on the **Notifications** tab

  Notifications   >

3 Tap on the items under the **Include** section to add items to appear in the Notification Center, under the **Today** heading

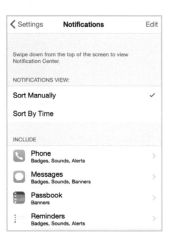

Hot tip

To enable email messages from your iCloud mail to appear in the Notifications Center, select the Mail app in Step 3 and tap on the **iCloud** button. On the next screen, drag the **Show in Notification Center** button to **On**.

4 Drag the **Allow Notifications** button to **On** to enable the select app to display notification in the Notifications Center

5 Select options for the notification sound and icon and select whether you want to show it on the Lock Screen or not

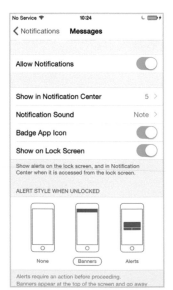

...cont'd

Once the Notification Center settings have been selected, it can be used to keep up-to-date with all of your important appointments and reminders. It can also be used to display the weather for your current location. To view the Notification Center from any screen:

 Drag down from the top of any screen to view the Notification Center. Tap on the **Today** button to view the Weather summary, Calendar items, Reminder items, stock market information and a summary of items for the next day

To change the items that appear in the **Today** view, swipe to the bottom of the screen and tap on the **Edit** button to delete options.

 Swipe up the page to view all of the items. Tap on one to open it in its own default app

131

Swipe up on this button to close the Notification Center.

 Tap on the **Notifications** button to view notifications from all of the selected apps in Steps 3 and 4 on the previous page

More Apps

Weather

This app tells you what the weather forecast is for the next six days. You can program the app to show the weather in multiple places. You can also choose between Centigrade or Fahrenheit.

Stocks

The Stocks app makes it easy to see how your stocks and shares are doing, both numerically and graphically.

Calculator

As expected, this is a fully-functioning calculator. You can view a standard calculator if you view in portrait mode. However, if you rotate the screen to landscape, the calculator changes to a scientific calculator.

Clock

This app functions as a clock, alarm, stop watch and timer. You can see what time it is in any city in the world by adding these to your clock screen.

Passbook

This stores your boarding passes and other coupons. You need to purchase additional software using the App Store to make Passbook fully functional and it does not work in all geographic locations.

Compass

The compass needs to be calibrated before you use it – tilt the iPhone to do this. The red needle points to north and you can find your current location by allowing the compass to use your location when you start using it.

iTunes Store

This is the iPhone version of the iTunes store on the Mac or PC. You can buy audio and video content for your iPhone.

Voice Memos

The iPhone is a great voice recorder. You can make voice notes for yourself then email them to colleagues or yourself to listen to later.

In iOS 8 there is also a **Tips** app which contains visual information about using iOS 8 and some of the apps in it. This information is updated on a regular basis.

7 Web Browsing

Browsing the web on the iPhone is very

easy using Apple's inbuilt browser, Safari.

This chapter looks at how to use Safari,

navigate around web pages, save and

organize bookmarks and use live links

within web pages.

Wi-Fi and Bluetooth drain battery power. Switch off when not required.

Network Connections

Your iPhone can download data, such as emails and web pages, using a number of different types of connection. Some types of connection are faster than others. In general, Wi-Fi and Bluetooth should be kept off if you are not using them because they use a considerable amount of power.

GPRS
This is a slow network! But often better than nothing.

EDGE
This is a relatively slow connection but is fine for email.

3G and 4G
These are faster connections than EDGE. 4G is pretty close to Wi-Fi speed.

Wi-Fi connection
Joining a wireless connection will give you fairly fast download speeds. There are many free Wi-Fi hotspots. You can use home Wi-Fi once you enter the password.

Bluetooth
This is a short-range wireless connection, generally used for communication using a Bluetooth headset.

What do the various icons mean?
Look at the top of the iPhone and you will see various icons relating to cellular and other networks.

●●●●○	Signal strength
O2-UK	Network provider
🛜	Wi-Fi On, with good signal strength
✳	Bluetooth On
✈	Airplane mode On
☼	iPhone is busy connecting, or getting mail, or some other task which has not completed

Configuring Networks

Wi-Fi

 1 Go to **Settings > Wi-Fi**

 2 Tap **Wi-Fi**

 3 Tap **On** if it is off

 4 Choose a **network** from those listed and enter the password

5 Tap **Ask to Join Networks** if you want to be prompted each time a new network is found. It's generally easier to leave this **Off**

6 If you want to forget the network (e.g. maybe you have used one in a hotel), tap the name of the network you have joined, and tap **Forget This Network**

Hot tip

Use Wi-Fi when available to save your data usage from the network provider.

No Service 🛜	10:54	🔋⚡
❮ Settings	**Wi-Fi**	

Wi-Fi	⬤
✓ PlusnetWireless792287	🔒 🛜 ⓘ

CHOOSE A NETWORK...

virginmedia6249958	🔒 🛜 ⓘ
Other...	

Ask to Join Networks	◯

Known networks will be joined automatically. If no known networks are available, you will have to manually select a network.

No Service 🛜	10:54	🔋⚡
❮ Wi-Fi	**PlusnetWireless792287**	

Forget This Network

IP ADDRESS

DHCP	BootP	Static

IP Address	192.168.1.122
Subnet Mask	255.255.255.0
Router	192.168.1.254
DNS	192.168.1.254
Search Domains	lan
Client ID	

Renew Lease

HTTP PROXY

Off	Manual	Auto

Browse with Safari

The Safari app is the default web browser on the iPhone. This can be used to view web pages, save favorites and read pages with the Reader function. To start using Safari:

 Tap on the **Safari** app

 Tap on the Address Bar at the top of the Safari window. Type a web page address

 Tap on the **Go** button on the keyboard to open the web page

4 Also, suggested options appear as you type. Tap on one of these to go to that page

 The selected web page opens in Safari

When a page opens in Safari a blue status bar underneath the page name indicates the progress of the loading page.

6 Swipe up and down and left and right to navigate around the page

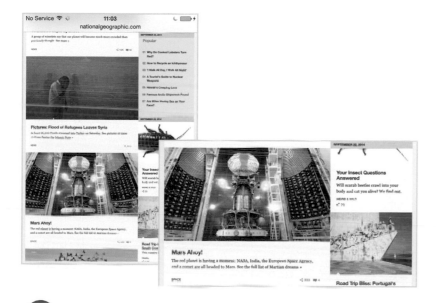

Double-tap with one finger to zoom in on a page by a set amount. Double-tap with one finger to return to normal view. If the page has been zoomed by a greater amount by pinching, double-tap with two fingers to return to normal view.

7 Swipe outwards with thumb and forefinger to zoom in on a web page (pinch inwards to zoom back out)

Wild Bears in Alaska

In case you missed it: See stunnin footage of bears in America's larg

Zooming and Scrolling

Because of the small screen, there is a limit to how much of the web page you can see.

Scroll
Place your finger on the screen and drag up or down, and left or right.

Zoom

 Place your index and middle finger on the screen

 Push them apart to zoom in

 Pinch them together to zoom out

You can also zoom in by placing your thumb and forefinger on the screen and pushing them apart (pinch them inwards to zoom out again).

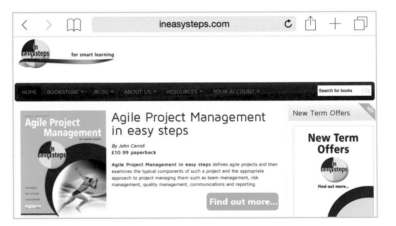

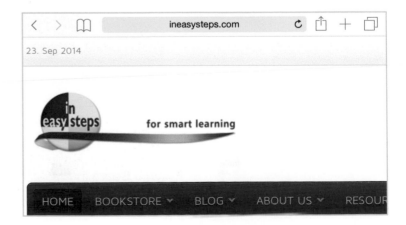

Scroll up to the top of a page to activate the top address bar and the bottom toolbar when you tap on the page.

Add Web Clip to Home Screen

If you find a site that you want to revisit, but not add to bookmarks, you can add it to the Home screen:

1 Open the required web page

Add regularly-visited websites to your Home screen to save you having to look for the bookmark.

2 Tap on the **Share** button and tap on the **Add to Home Screen** button

3 Give the page a name and tap on the **Add** button

4 The web clip is added to the Home screen as an icon

Navigating Pages

When you are viewing pages within Safari there are a number of functions that can be used:

1 Tap on these buttons to move forward and back between web pages that have been visited

2 Tap here to view Bookmarked pages, Reading List pages and Shared Links

3 Tap here to add a bookmark, add to a reading list, add an icon to your iPhone Home screen, email a link to a page, Tweet a page, send it to Facebook or print a page

4 Tap here to add a new tab

5 Tap on a link on a page to open it. Tap and hold to access additional options, to open in a new tab, add to a Reading List or copy the link

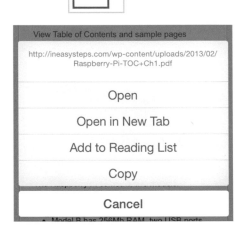

6 Tap and hold on an image and tap on **Save Image** or **Copy**

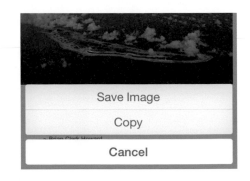

Opening New Tabs

Safari supports tabbed browsing, which means that you can open separate pages within the same window and access them by tapping on each tab at the top of the page:

1 Tap here to view the open tab

2 The open tabs are displayed. Tap on one to go to that tab

Hot tip

Tap on the **Private** button in the tabs window to open an inPrivate browsing session, where no web details will be recorded.

3 Tap on this button at the bottom of the window to create a new tab

4 Tap on the cross on a tab to close it

5 Open a new tab from Step 3 by entering a web address into the Address Bar, or tap on one of the thumbnails in the **Favorites** window

Hot tip

The items that appear in the Favorites window can be determined within **Settings > Safari** and tapping once on the **Favorites** link.

Bookmarking Pages

Once you start using Safari you will soon build up a collection of favorite pages that you visit regularly. To access these quickly they can be bookmarked so that you can then go to them in one tap. To set up and use bookmarks:

 Open a web page that you want to bookmark. Tap once here to access the sharing options

 Tap on the **Add Bookmark** button

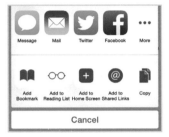

The Favorites Bar appears underneath the Address Bar in Safari. This includes items that have been added as bookmarks.

 Tap on this link and select whether to include the bookmark on the Favorites Bar or in a Bookmarks folder

 Tap on the **Save** button

 Tap on the **Bookmarks** button

 Tap here on the **Bookmarks** button to view all of the bookmarks. The Bookmarks folders are listed. Tap on the **Edit** button to delete or rename the folders

Reading List and Shared Links

The button in Step 5 on the previous page can be used to access your Reading List and Shared Links.

Reading List
This is a list of web pages that have been saved for reading at a later date. The great thing about this function is that the pages can be read even when you are offline and not connected to the Internet.

1 Tap on this button to view your **Reading List**

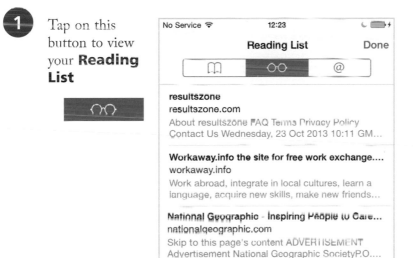

Reading List items can be added from the Share button in Step 1 on the previous page.

Shared Links
If you have added a Twitter account on your iPhone you will be able to view your updates from the Shared Links button.

1 Tap on this button to view your **Shared Links** updates

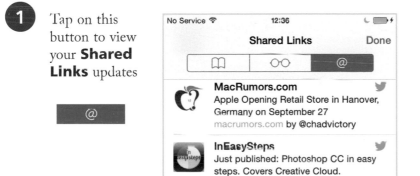

If you have accounts with Facebook or Twitter, you can link to these from the left-hand panel of the **Settings** app. Once you have done this you can share content to these sites from apps on your iPhone.

Safari Settings

Settings for Safari can be specified in the Settings app. To do this:

 Tap on the **Settings** app

 Tap on the **Safari** tab Safari

 Tap on the **Search Engine** link to select a default search engine to use

‹ Settings	**Safari**	
SEARCH		
Search Engine		Google ›
Search Engine Suggestions		⬤
Spotlight Suggestions		⬤
Quick Website Search		On ›
Preload Top Hit		⬤

 Tap on the default search engine you want to use with Safari

144

Beware

Don't use **Autofill** for names and passwords for any sites with sensitive information, such as banking sites, if other people have access to the iPhone.

5 Tap here for options for filling in online forms

Passwords & AutoFill	›

6 Tap on this button to access options for opening new links on a web site

Open Links	In New Tab ›

7 Tap on this button to access options for the Favorites window that appears when you open a new tab

Favorites	Favorites ›

8 Drag the **Do Not Track** button to **Off** to disable this. If tracking is Off then no information will be recorded about visited websites

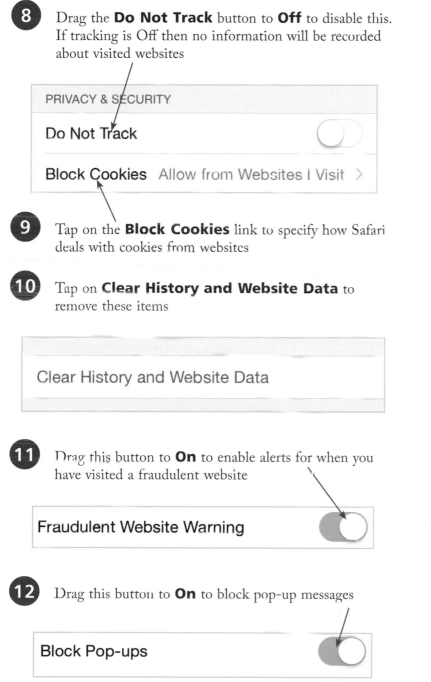

PRIVACY & SECURITY

Do Not Track

Block Cookies   Allow from Websites I Visit >

9 Tap on the **Block Cookies** link to specify how Safari deals with cookies from websites

10 Tap on **Clear History and Website Data** to remove these items

Clear History and Website Data

11 Drag this button to **On** to enable alerts for when you have visited a fraudulent website

Fraudulent Website Warning

12 Drag this button to **On** to block pop-up messages

Block Pop-ups

Cookies are small items from websites that obtain details from your browser when you visit a site. The cookie remembers the details for the next time you visit the site.

If the **History** is cleared then there will be no record of any sites that have been visited.

Tricks

Fast Safari Scrolling

You can scroll up and down through web pages in Safari using your finger to flick up and down. But there is a very quick way of getting to the top of any web page.

Tap the time! (this works with text messages, and other apps like Facebook, too).

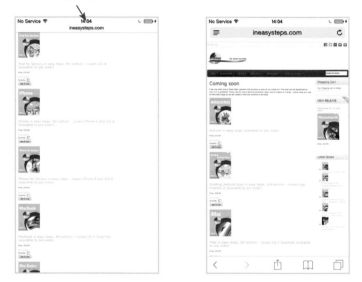

Keyboard shortcuts when entering URLs

You don't need to type *.co.uk* or *.com*. On the Safari keyboard, press and hold the *period* key. Alternatives will pop up.

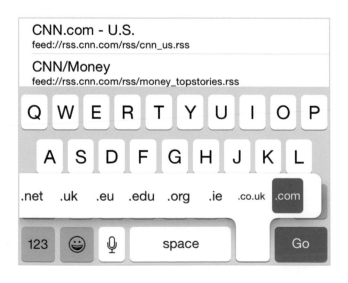

8 Email

Most of us spend a great deal of time reading and composing emails. This chapter looks at how to set up email on your iPhone so that you can send and receive emails with your friends, family and colleagues.

Setting Up Email

The iPhone handles email well, and works with iCloud and Microsoft Exchange. It handles POP3, IMAP and can work with Yahoo! Mail, Google Mail and AOL.

Setting up an email account

You can link to a variety of email accounts and this example uses a Gmail account:

 Go to **Settings > Mail, Contacts, Calendars**

 Tap on the **Add Account** button

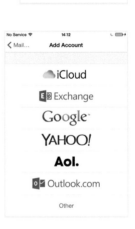 Select the account you want to add (in this case Google)

 Enter the account details and tap on the **Next** button

 Select the items you want to include in the account and tap on the **Save** button

...cont'd

Deleting an account

To delete an email account from your iPhone:

1 Go to **Settings > Mail, Contacts, Calendars**

2 Tap on the account you want to delete

> No Service 📶 14:14 🔋➕
> ❮ Settings **Mail, Contacts, Calendars**
>
> ACCOUNTS
>
> **iCloud** >
> Mail, Contacts, Calendars, Safari and 7 more...
>
> **Gmail** >
> Mail, Contacts, Calendars, Notes
>
> **Add Account** >
>
> Fetch New Data   Push >
>
> MAIL
>
> Preview   2 Lines >
>
> Show To/Cc Label   ⚪
>
> Swipe Options   >
>
> Flag Style   Color >
>
> Ask Before Deleting   ⚪
>
> Load Remote Images   🟢

3 In the account window, swipe down to the bottom of the screen and tap on the **Delete Account** button and then the **Delete from My iPhone** button

> No Service 📶 14:14 🔋➕
> ❮ Mail... **Gmail**
>
> GMAIL
>
> Account   nickvandome@gmail.com >
>
> ✉ Mail   🟢
>
> 👤 Contacts   🟢
>
> 📅 Calendars   🟢
>
> 📄 Notes   🟢
>
> Delete Account

149

Using Exchange Server

Mail can collect email, and sync calendars and contacts using Microsoft Exchange Server, which is great news for businesses. To do this:

 Go to **Settings > Mail, Contacts, Calendars**

 Tap on the **Exchange** button

 Enter the details of your Exchange account (you may need to get these from your IT Administrator) and tap on the **Next** button

Email Viewing Settings

As with other apps, there are a number of settings for email:

 Go to **Settings > Mail, Contacts, Calendars**

 Tap on one of the accounts to view its settings

 Adjust settings for **Preview**, **Ask Before Deleting**, **Show To/Cc Label**, etc.

 Access **Settings > General > Accessibility > Larger Text** to change the text size

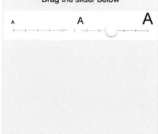

Hot tip

If you want to see more text on the screen set the font size to small.

Composing Email

You can keep in touch with everyone, straight from the Mail app:

 Tap the **Mail** icon to open the app

 Tap an **email account** to open it

 Tap the **New Email** icon (bottom right). A new email will open

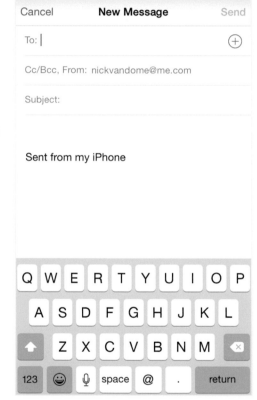

 Tap the **To:** field and type the name of the recipient

 Tap the **Subject:** and enter a subject for the email

 Tap the **email body** area (below Subject:) and start typing your email

 Insert a photo by pressing and holding in the body of the email and selecting **Insert Photo or Video** from the pop-up menu and then select a photo from your photo gallery

 Once complete, hit **Send**

Reading Email

When you receive email you can view it in the Mail app:

1 Check the **Mail** icon for fresh mail – represented by a red circle. The number refers to the number of unread emails

2 Tap **Mail** to open

3 Tap the **Inbox** to open the email and if there is blue dot next to an email it means that it is unread

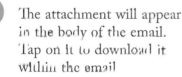

Hot tip

Flag important emails so you can find them again easily. Swipe from right to left on the email and tap on the **Flag** button.

4 If there is an attachment for the email this will be indicated by a paperclip icon next to it – you can tap to download

5 The attachment will appear in the body of the email. Tap on it to download it within the email

Beware

Often, attachments do not download automatically. Tap the icon and you will see the attachment downloading. After downloading, tap to open.

6 When the image attachment has finished downloading it will be visible in the body of the email

Hot tip

To save a photo from an email, press and hold on the photo until you see **Save Image.** Tap on this, and the photo will be added to the **Photos** section of the **Photos** app.

Forwarding Email

Once you have received an email you can reply to the sender, or forward it to someone else:

1 Open an email

2 Tap the **Reply/ Forward** icon at the bottom right of the screen

3 Select **Forward**

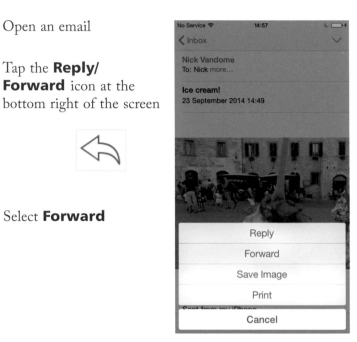

4 Enter the name of the recipient in the **To** box

5 In the body of the email, enter any message you want to accompany the forwarded email

6 Tap on the **Send** button

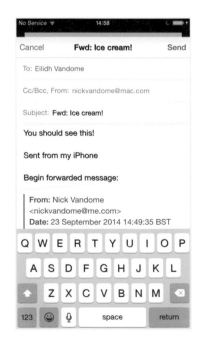

Deleting Email

You can delete email a couple of different ways

 Tap the email to read it

 When finished, tap the trash icon at the bottom of the screen

Alternative method

 In the email list view slide your finger across the email from right to left (do not open it)

A red **Trash** box should appear

Tap **Trash** and the email will be deleted

There are also options in the Trash option to **Flag** the email and a **More** button, from which you can reply, forward, mark or move the email.

155

Yet another way of deleting email is

 Go to **Inbox** and tap the **Edit** button at the top right

The contents of the Inbox are displayed in Edit mode

Tap each email you want to delete and a blue circle will appear in the left column

Hit **Trash** when you are ready to delete

Move Email to Folders

If you have an IMAP account, such as an iCloud account, you can see your folders on the server. You can move mail from your Inbox to another folder. This helps keep your mail organized, and your Inbox uncluttered.

1 Open the email you want to move and tap on the **Folder** button on the bottom toolbar

2 Tap on the folder into which you want to move the email. In this instance, it is **Family**

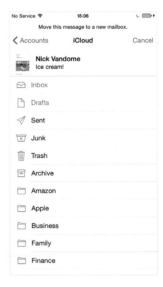

3 The email appears in the selected folder

9 Accessibility Settings

The iPhone is well suited for people with visual or motor issues. This chapter details the Accessibility options on the iPhone, so that everyone can get the most out of it.

Accessibility Settings

Many people with visual impairments should be able to make use of devices like the iPhone. With the standard default configuration they may run into problems, but the iPhone has many settings that can be modified to make them more usable.

What features are available?

- VoiceOver

- Zoom

- White on Black

- Mono Audio

- Speak Auto-text

Most of these features will work with most applications, apart from VoiceOver which will only work with the iPhone's standard (pre-installed) applications.

 Tap on the **Settings** app

 Tap on the **General** tab

 Tap on the **Accessibility** link

 The **Accessibility** options are displayed – tap on a link to access more options

...cont'd

5 Or, drag the button **On** or **Off** to access these

No Service 📶   15:20   🌙 🔋⚡

‹ Accessibility   **VoiceOver**

VoiceOver

VoiceOver speaks items on the screen:
- Tap once to select an item
- Double-Tap to activate the selected item
- Swipe three fingers to scroll

SPEAKING RATE

Speak Hints

Use Pitch Change

Use Sound Effects

Speech   ›

Braille   ›

6 Swipe up and down the page to view the full range of options for each item

No Service 📶   15:20   🌙 🔋⚡

‹ Accessibility   **VoiceOver**

Use Pitch Change

Use Sound Effects

Speech   ›

Braille   ›

Rotor   ›

Typing Style   Standard Typing ›

Phonetic Feedback   Character and Pho... ›

Typing Feedback   ›

Always Speak Notifications

Navigate Images   Always ›

Large Cursor

159

Activate Settings on iPhone

Switching on VoiceOver

 1 Go to **Settings** > **General** > **Accessibility**

2 Activate **VoiceOver** as shown below

3 When finished, you may wish to switch it off again

Tap on VoiceOver and drag the button on to activate it

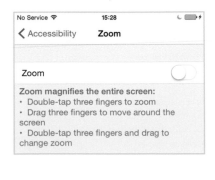

Switch to Zoom to enlarge (Zoom cannot be used with VoiceOver)

VoiceOver

VoiceOver
This speaks what's on the screen, so you can tell what's on the screen even if you cannot see it. It describes items on the screen and, if text is selected, VoiceOver will read the text.

Speaking rate
This can be adjusted using the settings.

Typing feedback
VoiceOver can provide this: go to **Settings > General > Accessibility > VoiceOver > Typing Feedback**.

Languages
VoiceOver is available in languages other than English (but is not available in all languages).

VoiceOver Gestures
When VoiceOver is active, the standard touch screen gestures operate differently:

Tap	Speak item
Flick right or left	Select next or previous item
Flick up or down	Depends on Rotor Control setting
Two-finger tap	Stop speaking current item
Two-finger flick up	Read all from top of screen
Two-finger flick down	Read all from current position
Three-finger flick up or down	Scroll one page at a time
Three-finger flick right or left	Go to next or previous page
Three-finger tap	Speak the scroll status

Apple Support for VoiceOver
See: **http://support.apple.com/kb/HT3598**

Zoom

The iPhone touch screen lets you zoom in and out of elements on the screen. Zoom will let you magnify the whole screen, irrespective of which application you are running.

Turn Zoom on and off

 Go to **Settings > General > Accessibility > Zoom**

 Tap the Zoom **Off/On** switch

 You cannot use Zoom and VoiceOver at the same time

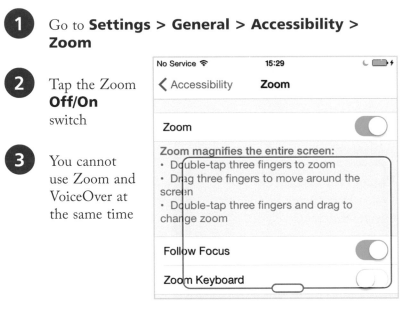

Zoom in and out

 Double tap the screen with three fingers

 The screen will then magnify by 200%

Increase magnification

 Use **three fingers** and drag to the top of the screen (increase magnification) or bottom (decrease magnification)

 Move around the screen

 Drag or flick the screen with three fingers

Other Accessibility Settings

Activate Increase Contrast

This feature enhances the contrast on the iPhone, which may make it easier for some people to read.

 Go to **Settings > General > Accessibility**

 Tap the **Increase Contrast** link

 Drag the **Reduce Transparency** button to **On**

Turn Mono Audio on and off

This combines the sound of both left and right channels into a mono audio signal played through both sides.

 Go to **Settings > General > Accessibility**

 Switch on **Mono Audio**

Turn Speak Auto-text on

This setting enables the iPhone to speak text corrections and suggestions as you type text into the iPhone.

 Go to **Settings > General > Accessibility**

 Select **Speech** and switch on **Speak Auto-text**

 Speak Auto-text works with VoiceOver and Zoom

Large phone keypad

The keypad of the iPhone is large, making it easy for people who are visually impaired to see the digits.

 Tap the **Phone** icon (on the dock)

 Tap the **keypad** icon (4th icon from left)

Closed Captioning adds subtitles to video content. Not all videos contain Closed Captioning information but where it is available you can access it by turning on Closed Captions.

Restrictions

If children are going to be using your iPhone, or if they have their own, you may want to restrict the type of content they can access:

1 Tap on the **Settings** app

2 Tap on the **General** tab

General

3 Tap on the **Restrictions** link

| Restrictions | Off > |

4 By default the restrictions are disabled, i.e. grayed-out so they cannot be accessed. Tap on the **Enable Restrictions** button

❮ General   **Restrictions**

Enable Restrictions

ALLOW:

🧭 Safari

5 Set a passcode in order to set restrictions

Set Passcode   Cancel

Enter a Restrictions Passcode

● ● ● —

6 For the items you want to restrict, drag their buttons to **Off**. These icons will no longer appear on the iPhone's Home screen

❮ General   **Restrictions**

Disable Restrictions

ALLOW:

🧭 Safari

📷 Camera

📹 FaceTime

🎙 Siri

Beware

If you are restricting items for someone, make sure that you discuss it with them and explain your reasons for doing this, rather than just letting them find out for themselves when they try to use an app.

10 Working with Apps

There are thousands of apps for the iPhone, catering for every conceivable need. This chapter looks at how to find apps in the online App Store, install them, update them and remove them.

Organizing Apps

When you start downloading apps you will probably soon find that you have dozens, if not hundreds, of them. You can move between screens to view all of your apps by swiping left or right with one finger.

Hot tip

To move an app between screens, tap and hold on it until it starts to jiggle and a cross appears in the corner. Then drag it to the side of the screen. If there is space on the next screen the app will be moved there.

As more apps are added it can become hard to find the apps you want, particularly if you have to swipe between several screens. However, it is possible to organize apps into individual folders to make using them more manageable.
To do this:

 Press on an app until it starts to jiggle and a blue cross appears at the top-left corner. (This can be used to delete the app unless it is a preinstalled app, in which case the cross does not appear)

 Drag the app over another one

3 A folder is created, containing the two apps. The folder is given a default name, usually based on the category of the apps

4 Tap on the folder name and type a new name if required

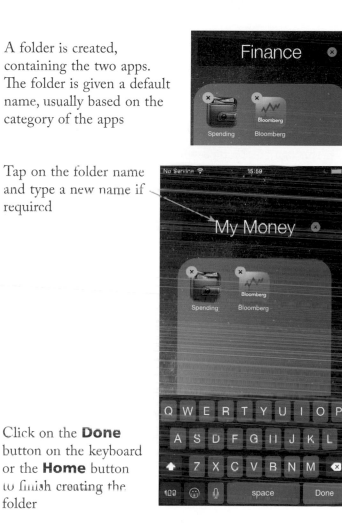

5 Click on the **Done** button on the keyboard or the **Home** button to finish creating the folder

6 Click the **Home** button again to return to the Home screen (this is done whenever you want to return to the Home screen from an apps folder)

7 The folder is added on the Home screen. Tap on this to access the items within it

Beware

Only top-level folders can be created, i.e. sub-folders cannot be created. Also, one folder cannot be placed within another.

167

Hot tip

If you want to rename an apps folder after it has been created, tap and hold on it until it starts to jiggle. Then tap on the folder name and edit it as in Steps 4 and 5.

About the App Store

While the built-in apps that come with the iPhone are flexible and versatile, it really comes into its own when you connect to the App Store. This is an online resource and there are thousands of apps there that can be downloaded and then used on your iPhone, including categories from Lifestyle to Travel and Medical.

To use the App Store, you must first have an Apple ID (see page 32). This can be obtained when you first connect to the App Store. Once you have an Apple ID you can start exploring the App Store:

 Tap on the **App Store** app on the Home screen

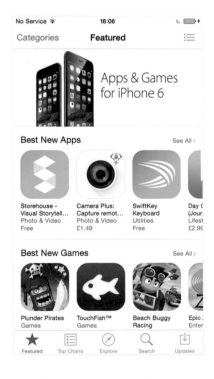 The latest available apps are displayed on the homepage of the App Store, including the Editor's Choice, featured in the top panel

Tap on these buttons to view the apps according to **Featured**, **Top Charts**, **Explore** and **Updates**

Viewing apps

To view apps in the App Store and read about their content and functionality:

 Tap once on an app

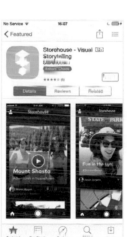 General details about the app are displayed

Swipe left or right here to view additional information about the app and view details

Reviews and **Related** apps are available from the relevant buttons, next to the **Details** button

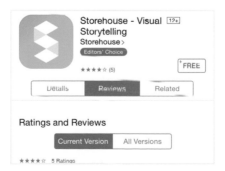

Finding Apps

Featured

Within the App Store, apps are separated into categories according to type. This enables you to find apps according to particular subjects. To do this:

 Tap on the **Featured** button on the toolbar at the bottom of the App Store

 Scroll left and right to view different category headings

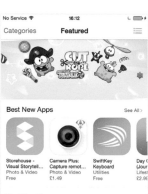

Tap on the **Categories** button to view apps in specific categories.

Scroll up the page to view additional categories and **Quick Links**

Top Charts

To find the top rating apps:

 Tap on the **Top Charts** button on the toolbar at the bottom of the App Store

 The top overall paid for, free and top grossing apps are displayed

There are now so many apps, it may be difficult to find what you want. Try using the search tool and enter a word or words that describe what you are looking for.

 To find the top apps in different categories, tap on the **Categories** button

Categories

Select a category

The top apps for that category are displayed

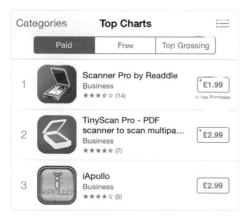

Do not limit yourself to just viewing the top apps. Although these are the most popular, there are also a lot of excellent apps within each category.

In the top of the Explore window is a **Popular Near Me** section that highlights apps that are relevant to your location.

...cont'd

Explore

This is a feature which suggests appropriate apps according to your current geographic location. To use this:

1 Tap once on the **Explore** button on the toolbar at the bottom of the App Store

2 Tap once on the **Allow** button to enable the App Store to use your location (**Location Services** have to be turned On)

> Allow "App Store" to access your location while you use the app?
> Your location is used to find relevant apps nearby.
>
> Don't Allow | Allow

3 Recommendations will appear in the **Explore** window, with category options in the left-hand panel

Explore
CATEGORIES
Books
Business
Catalogues
Education
Entertainment
Finance
Food & Drink
Games
Health & Fitness

4 Tap once on one of the categories to view specific apps for these

Searching for apps

Another way to find apps is with the App Store Search box,
which is located at the top-right corner of the App Store window.
To use this:

1 Tap on the **Search**
button at the
bottom of the
window to access
the **Search** box
and bring up the
iPhone virtual keyboard

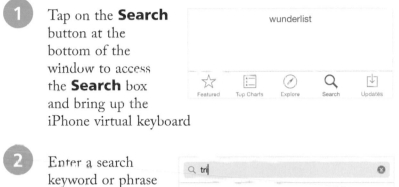

2 Enter a search
keyword or phrase

3 Suggested apps
appear as you are
typing

4 Tap on an app to view it

Installation Process

To install apps from the App Store:

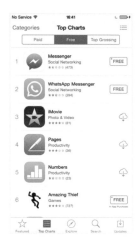

1 Find the app you want using **App Store** on the iPhone

2 Tap the **Price** or **Free** tab

3 Tap on the **Install** button

4 Enter your iTunes password

5 The app will install

Updating Apps

The publishers of apps provide updates which bring new features and improvements. You don't have to check your apps to see if there are updates – you can set them to be updated automatically through the Settings app. To do this:

1 Open **Settings** and tap on the **iTunes & App Store** link

Ⓐ	iTunes & App Store	>

No Service 🗚 16:42

Settings

🔲	Touch ID & Passcode	>
✋	Privacy	>
☁	iCloud nickvandome@mac.com	>
Ⓐ	iTunes & App Store	>
✉	Mail, Contacts, Calendars	>
📝	Notes	>
☰	Reminders	>
📞	Phone	>
💬	Messages	>
📷	FaceTime	>
📍	Maps	>
🧭	Compass	>

2 Drag the **Updates** button to **On** to enable automatic updates for apps

Ⓐ	Updates	⬤

No Service 🗚 16:43

< Settings   **iTunes & App Store**

SHOW ALL

Music	⬤
Videos	⬤

Show all store purchases and iTunes Match uploads in your music and video libraries, even if they have not been downloaded to this iPhone.

Subscribe to iTunes Match

Store all your music in iCloud with iTunes Match. Learn more...

AUTOMATIC DOWNLOADS

🎵	Music	◯
Ⓐ	Apps	⬤
📖	Books	⬤
Ⓐ	Updates	⬤

Automatically download new purchases (including free) made on other devices.

Hot tip

If your App Store icon has a red circle with a number inside, it means there's an update for one or more of your apps. If updates are not set to automatic, the apps can be updated manually in the **Updates** section of the App Store.

Removing Apps

To remove apps from your iPhone (excluding preinstalled ones):

 Press and hold the app you want to remove

 All the apps on the screen will start jiggling and you will see an **x** at the top of the app unless it cannot be removed, i.e. it is a preinstalled app such as Phone, Mail, Calendar, etc. (see page 19)

3 Tap the **x** and the app will be deleted

4 Tap on the **Delete** button to confirm your action

Don't forget

If you remove an app, it can be reinstalled from the App Store. The app will have a cloud icon next to it and will be free to reinstall, even if it was a paid-for app.

11 Solving Problems

The iPhone occasionally misbehaves — an app will not close, or the iPhone may malfunction. This section looks at how to fix common problems and provides some helpful websites. The chapter also helps you find your lost or stolen iPhone.

General iPhone Care

The iPhone is a fairly robust gadget but, like any complex piece of electronic hardware, it may suffer from knocks, scratches, getting wet and other problems.

Cleaning the body and screen

The touch screen is supposed to be scratch resistant. In fact, there are YouTube videos showing people trying to scratch the screen by placing the iPhone into a plastic bag containing keys and shaking the whole thing around. Amazingly, the screen seems not to scratch. Then they put it in a blender and it, well, got blended. So it's definitely not blender-proof!

Hot tip

Paper kitchen towel, dampened with a little water containing a couple of drops of dishwashing liquid, is great for getting rid of heavily greased screens.

The best way to clean an iPhone is with a lint-free cloth such as the one above used for cleaning reading glasses. Make sure there is no grit or sand on the body or screen and gently rub with the cleaning cloth. This should bring back the shine without scratching the glass or the back of the phone.

Occasionally the screen may get very greasy and a little soap helps to get the grease off

 1 Put a few drops of dishwashing liquid in warm water

 2 Get some paper kitchen towel and dip this into the water

 3 Wring out the kitchen towel so it is not dripping wet and lightly wipe over the screen and rest of the casing

 4 Dry off using a clean cloth

Keep iPhone Up-to-Date

Apple releases updates to the iPhone operating system periodically.

Is your iPhone fully up-to-date?

 Tap on the **Settings** app

 Tap on the **General** tab

Tap on the **Software Update** link to view the current status of your operating system

Software updates for iPhone users are provided free by Apple. If one becomes available, download and install it.

If there is an update available it will be displayed

Tap on the **Download and Install** button

179

Maximize iPhone Battery

The iPhone is a bit of a power hog. Browsing the web, listening to music and watching videos drains power. If you only make a few phone calls each day, your iPhone will last a couple of days between charges. But most people use it for far more than this and their battery will last about a day.

Tweaks to ensure maximum battery life

Hot tip

You can conserve battery power by switching off Wi-Fi and Bluetooth. Instead of opting for push email, you can check for email manually.

1 Switch Off **Wi-Fi** if you don't need it

2 Switch Off **Bluetooth** if you don't need it

3 Switch On **Battery Percentage** indicator, under **Settings > General > Usage**

4 Switch off **3G/4G** if you don't need this, under **Settings > Cellular (Mobile)**

5 Collect your **email manually**, under **Mail, Contacts, Calendars > Fetch New Data**

6 Set **Auto-lock** to a short period, e.g. 1 minute, under **Settings > General > Auto-Lock**

7 Always hit the **Off** button when you have finished using the iPhone (screen goes black which uses less power)

Beware

If you use Airplane Mode you will not receive any calls, texts or notifications.

8 Reduce the brightness of your screen, under **Settings > Display & Brightness**

9 Consider using **Airplane Mode** for maximum conservation of power!

Restart, Force Quit and Reset

Restart the iPhone
If the iPhone misbehaves, or applications act strangely, you can restart the iPhone.

 Hold down the Sleep/Wake button

 When you see the **Slide to Power Off** appear, **swipe this to the right**

 Leave the iPhone for a couple of minutes then press the **Sleep/Wake** button again and let the phone restart

Quit an app
Sometimes apps misbehave and you want to quit them and reopen. To do this, press the Home button twice to access the multitasking window.

Swipe left or right to find the app that you want to quit and swipe it up to the top of the screen.

Force Quit the iPhone

 Press the **Sleep/Wake** and the **Home button** at the same time

 The screen will suddenly turn black and the iPhone will automatically restart

...cont'd

Resetting the iPhone

There are various aspects of your iPhone that can be reset to their factory defaults. These include resetting the Home Screen Layout, Network Settings and the Keyboard Dictionary. You can also reset all of the settings on the iPhone, or the Content and Settings. This erases all of the content and resets the iPhone to its factory, unused, condition. You may want to do this if you have been using the iPhone and then want to give it to someone else. To do this:

 Select **Settings > General** and tap on the **Reset** button (at the bottom of the page)

Reset	>

② All of the Reset options are displayed. Tap on the **Erase All Content and Settings** button

‹ General	**Reset**
Reset All Settings	
Erase All Content and Settings	
Reset Network Settings	
Reset Keyboard Dictionary	
Reset Home Screen Layout	
Reset Location & Privacy	

③ Enter a passcode if you use one to lock your iPhone

Enter Passcode	Cancel

Enter your passcode

● ● ● —

4 Tap on the **Erase iPhone** button

This will delete all media and data, and reset all settings.

Erase iPhone

Cancel

5 Since it is a serious action you will be asked if you are sure. Tap on the **Erase iPhone** button again

Are you sure you want to continue? All media, data, and settings will be erased. This cannot be undone.

Erase iPhone

Cancel

6 Enter your Apple ID and tap on the **Erase** button to return your iPhone to its factory condition

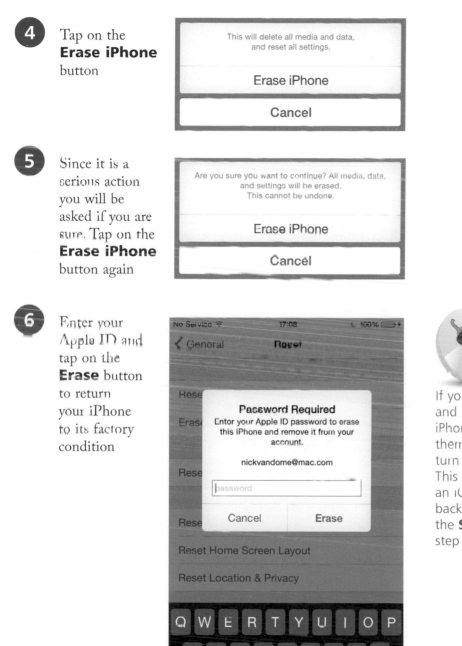

No Service 🔋 17:08 100% ⬛ ⚡

‹ General   Reset

Rese

Password Required

Eras Enter your Apple ID password to erase this iPhone and remove it from your account.

nickvandome@mac.com

Rese password

Cancel   Erase

Rese

Reset Home Screen Layout

Reset Location & Privacy

Q W E R T Y U I O P

A S D F G H J K L

⬆ Z X C V B N M ⌫

.?123   space   return

Hot tip

If you reset the contents and settings for your iPhone you can restore them when you next turn on the phone. This can be done from an iCloud or an iTunes backup and is done at the **Set Up iPhone** step of the setup process.

183

The first place to look for hints, tips and fixes is Apple's website, which is chock full of information and videos.

Apple Resources

Visit Apple!
The first place you should look for help is the Apple site. After all, iPhone is their creation so they should know more than anyone.

The iPhone and iPhone Support areas are packed with information, tutorials and videos.

Useful URLs
http://www.apple.com/iphone/

http://www.apple.com/support/iphone/

David Pogue's posts
David Pogue is always worth reading – he loves technology and loves all things Apple. Try his own website at:

http://davidpogue.com/

or his New York Times blog at

http://pogue.blogs.nytimes.com/

iLounge
iLounge has long provided loads of hints and tips for Apple devices. These guys review hardware, accessories and provide reviews of new gear for the iPhone, the iPad and the iPod.

I Use This
Provides reviews of iPhone apps, and lets you know how many people are actually using the apps.

What's on iPhone
Largely a review site but it also provides information about hardware and for people interested in developing for the iPhone.

If You Lose Your iPhone

If you have lost or missplaced your iPhone you use iCloud to look for its location. The iPhone has to be on, and transmitting to the cellular network, in order for Find My iPhone to work.

Find My iPhone also allows you to erase the entire contents of your iPhone remotely. This means that if it gets stolen, you can remotely erase the iPhone and prevent whoever stole your iPhone from getting their hands on your personal data.

Set up Find My iPhone
Before you use Find My iPhone it has to be set up. To do this:

 Within Settings tap on the **iCloud** tab

 Tap on the Find My iPhone link and if the **Find My iPhone** functionality is Off, drag the button to **On**

 Tap on the **Allow** button in the Find My iPhone dialog box to activate this functionality

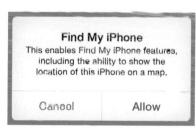

Hot tip

If for no other reason, it is worth getting an iCloud account so you can track your iPhone and erase the contents if it gets stolen.

Locating your iPhone
Once you have set up Find My iPhone you can then use the online service to locate it, lock it, or erase its contents.

 Log in to iCloud (**www.icloud.com**)

 Click on the **Find My iPhone** button

...cont'd

3 To use the Find My iPhone functionality you have to sign in again with your Apple ID

4 The location of your iPhone is shown on a map

5 Click on the **i** symbol to see options for your lost iPhone

Hot tip

The **Play Sound** option is a good one if you have lost the iPhone in your own home.

6 Details about the phone, and options for what you can do, are displayed

7 Click on the **Play Sound** button to send an alert sound to the phone. A message is displayed to let you know that a sound has been sent to your iPhone

8 Click on the **Lost Mode** button to lock your iPhone remotely. You have to enter a passcode to do this and this will be required to unlock the iPhone

Don't forget

Click on the **Erase iPhone > Erase** button if you are worried that someone might compromise the data on your iPhone

Index